EMERGENCY PREPAREDNESS FOR LIBRARIES

Julie Todaro

Government Institutes
An imprint of
The Scarecrow Press, Inc.
Lanham, Maryland • Toronto • Plymouth, UK
2009

1/09

 **Government Institutes**

Published in the United States of America
by Government Institutes, an imprint of The Scarecrow Press, Inc.
A wholly owned subsidiary of
The Rowman & Littlefield Publishing Group, Inc.
4501 Forbes Boulevard, Suite 200
Lanham, Maryland 20706
http://www.govinstpress.com/

Estover Road
Plymouth PL6 7PY
United Kingdom

British Library Cataloguing in Publication Information Available

Library of Congress Cataloging-in-Publication Data

Todaro, Julie Beth.
  Emergency preparedness for libraries / Julie Todaro.
    p.   cm.
  ISBN-13: 978-0-86587-166-3 (cloth : alk. paper)
  ISBN-10: 0-86587-166-3 (cloth : alk. paper)
  ISBN-13: 978-1-60590-274-6 (electronic : alk. paper)
  ISBN-10: 1-60590-274-8 (electronic : alk. paper)
  1. Libraries—Safety measures—Handbooks, manuals, etc.   2. Emergency
management   Planning—Handbooks, manuals, etc.   3. Library planning—
Handbooks, manuals, etc.   4. Library materials—Conservation and
restoration.
  I. Title.
  Z679.7.T63   2009
  025.8'2—dc22   2008041931

∞ ™ The paper used in this publication meets the minimum requirements of
American National Standard for Information Sciences—Permanence of Paper
for Printed Library Materials, ANSI/NISO Z39.48-1992. Manufactured in the
United States of America.

CONTENTS

DEDICATION

This book is dedicated to my mother, Phyllis, who supports me through all my projects with wisdom and humor; Madison, a great distraction and wonderful spaniel companion; and EB—a colleague whose considerable expertise in emergency management provided a much needed sounding board for ideas and much needed critical analysis.

INTRODUCTION

After many years in diverse library and information settings, I approach emergency and disaster discussions with some expertise. And although (luckily) I have not witnessed the massive destruction from floods and fires that some librarians have, but my observations and, sadly, real life experience comes from various levels of emergency and disaster situations—handling facilities, materials, resources, staff, and the public. Unfortunately I'm not alone—there probably isn't anyone managing a public facility today who can't also claim observation and direct experience with issues of prevention, the effects of contemporary disasters, and the struggles of recovery. Although the ranking or rating of a situation as a *disaster* or a particular *level* of disaster is the purview of a manager, one manager's minor situation may well be another manager's major event and should be treated and handled as such.

In addition to having experience in handling situations, I have also observed and experienced how others have handled them—unfortunately sometimes without a recommendation for action. Rather they included a fair share of "don't do this." I have generally made three observations: organizations with emergency and disaster plans are clearly ahead of those who don't have them; organizations that have talked about emergencies and how to prevent or minimize them as well as manage them are more aware of the *breadth* of what has to be done; and time and money spent in prevention is both time and money well spent.

~

Although the best way to prepare for both the foreseen and unforeseen is to have a complete disaster plan, including all supplies for any emergency and a myriad of communication strategies, the best approach is to take the "at the very least" approach. While this approach doesn't meet the needs of all possible circumstances, it is an important beginning and could even be labeled "right now" vs. "in the next year."

At the very least/right now:

- Managers should assess emergency management resources and opportunities available in their umbrella organizations.
- Managers should assess emergency management resources and opportunities in any partnership organizations.
- Managers should provide an "emergency awareness" training (that includes an organizational vulnerability self-assessment) for staff to provide them with the basics on protecting themselves and their constituents. This training should provide a forum for discussing vulnerability, the communication plan (in the following suggestion), and introducing the emergency kit for employees and constituents.
- All staff members should take part in the creation of a communication plan informing staff members and constituents in the building/on-site of any emergency situation. As part of this plan, sets of signs should be designed, produced, and stored for use in emergencies.
- Organizations should invest in emergency kits for staff members and constituents in the building for basic protection.
- Organizations should identify their data that is "unprotected"; that is, identify information that needs backup processes, du-

plication, and remote backup storage; managers should identify core data and data identified as organizational assets that need protection under any emergency condition.

In the next year:

- An employee work group should be created to address the ongoing handling of emergency content within the context of the umbrella institution (or partnership). This work group should:
  - Use data gathered from the initial training of organizational vulnerability self-assessment to address training and design of strategic emergency planning.
  - Design a plan to maintain processes to use umbrella organization data for complete disaster planning content.
  - Design a plan for updating and maintaining data and strategic plans as well as ongoing data protection.
  - Provide ongoing orientation, continuing education, and awareness of emergency issues, and unique and ongoing training for staff members and constituents in general as needed.
  - Provide ongoing orientation, continuing education, and awareness of emergency issues to staff and constituents with special needs.
  - Provide for constituent education in organizational planning.
- Organizations (the work group in combination with area managers and the umbrella institution) should assess emergency kit needs for staff members and constituents in the building/on-site for basic protection.
- Administration/management should assess budget planning for emergency management and request funds, if appropriate, for needs identified by work-group strategic planning.

While this monograph should assist you in planning for "at the very least/right now" and "in the next year," the content should also be helpful in looking at and planning for the bigger picture of emergency management and disaster planning. In fact, the best tools for the study of emergency management and disaster planning include the use of scenarios that introduce critical situations and problems and recommend the best practices for resolution. Scenarios are addressed differently throughout the text and begin with a formal process of steps and how those steps might be handled, including a list of steps specific to each scenario that are then proposed and employed. Institutions using the scenarios should consider beginning by addressing scenario elements to provide examples of critical thinking, problem-solving, and decision-making specific to emergency management and disaster recovery. Then educators or trainers should consider moving to the quicker, more informal process used in chapter 4. By using multiple ways to address scenarios, those needing training move from more structured critical thinking processes to establishing the critical questions and then offering answers.

❶

DEFINING TWENTY-FIRST CENTURY EMERGENCIES AND DISASTERS

CONTENTS

- Twenty-first Century Emergencies and Disasters
- Emergencies and Disasters
- Responses to Emergencies and Disasters: Today
- Responses to Emergencies and Disasters: Tomorrow/ Future
- Twenty-first Century Infrastructure: Organizations, Associations, and Commercial/Vendor
- Twenty-first Century Publications: Periodicals, Monographs, and The Online Environment
- Twenty-first Century Training, Continuing Education, and Professional Development
- Twenty-first Century Documents: Forms/Checklists

DEFINING TWENTY-FIRST CENTURY EMERGENCIES AND DISASTERS

Library and information environments project an image and "own" the stereotype of being quiet, calm, safe, and secure locations for staff members and constituents. The historical reality is, that libraries are not always safe and secure places to work or visit. Managers must embrace an area of management they are NOT used to—emergency management—and they must:

- Educate themselves on emergency management and emergency issues.
- Educate themselves not only on emergency prevention but also on related safety and security issues.
- Identify the emergency safety and security issues.
- Educate constituents.
- Establish policies that cover emergencies.
- Establish procedures that cover emergencies.
- Educate board, administration, peer managers, staff, volunteers, and city/country institutions on policies and procedures.

TWENTY-FIRST CENTURY EMERGENCIES AND DISASTERS

For decades, managers have been encountering unexpected situations and dealing with them in various ways. And although there is nothing "new" about the existence of these unexpected situations (or "emergencies and disasters") in work and work-related environments, the number and type of unexpected situations have changed as well as the ways of preparing for, dealing with, and following up in handling issues and future prevention.

Twenty-first century issues related to emergencies and disasters include the terms "emergencies" and "disasters" that are now typically used interchangeably; the literature in these areas that has grown exponentially; various umbrella terms, such as "emergency management" or "emergency preparedness"; public policy that has changed dramatically; human resources issues that have changed and grown; customer issues that have also changed and grown; and general preparedness and response policies and procedures.

Twenty-first century definitions of these terms also vary. *Emergency* and *disaster* definitions identify environment, such as "workplace" or work "environment," as separate from *home* emergencies and describe activities as *events* or accidents that are unanticipated as *unexpected* and/or *unforeseen*. Workplace events are characterized by whether they result or occur from man-made and natural factors that threaten the workforce and its constituents. This includes events that cause operations to cease, interrupting and possibly altering workflow or services to customers, and also includes the cause of damages to the physical, virtual, and digital workplace. Most definitions also include the impact on the organization and individuals working in the environment as well as those using services and resources provided by the organization.

Other twenty-first century issues include questions such as:

Are disasters occurring at a greater rate, in greater numbers and, if so, why? Why might some natural disasters also be categorized as man-made? What are the contemporary challenges to preparedness and prevention of disasters? What are preparedness and prevention elements?

Are disasters occurring at a greater rate, in greater numbers, and, if so, why?

Disasters are occurring at a greater rate and in greater numbers and, of course, we now know much more about the number and type of disasters happening everywhere given twenty-first century communications. Although there are many reasons for these changes (including climate change and land use mostly in developing countries), changing population patterns and increasing populations are thought to be the primary causes.

Why might some natural disasters also be categorized as man-made?

"Man's" use of natural resources, the changing nature and growth of cities, and diverse building patterns are just a few of the reasons why some disasters, historically thought of as natural, might now also be caused by man or considered "man-made."

What are the contemporary challenges to preparedness and prevention of disasters?

Preparedness and disaster prevention has always been and continues to be challenging. Although most people would identify the United States as a country that could always successfully respond to disasters, given recent natural and man-made disasters, this is no longer a commonly held belief. Challenges for all countries now include aging infrastructures, lack of funding, changing natural resources, lack of coordination among the stakeholders, and lack of designated partnerships as well as a lack of strategic planning, whether alone or cooperatively.

What are preparedness and prevention elements?

Although the basic elements of disasters have not changed appreciably over the past decades, certain elements are of more concern, depending on the disaster. For example, the impact of disasters has always been anticipated but now the impact on human beings is so much greater given contemporary knowledge of the medical and physical effects of disaster elements. Besides the human factor and immediate care, long-term care and rehabilitation, the social factor, the economic impact, and environmental impact are critical elements. Keeping this broad picture of the effects of disasters, the best preparedness and prevention elements include significant strategic planning.

Categorizing examples of emergencies and disasters used to include relatively clear-cut divisions between *natural* and *man-made*. In twenty-first century emergency preparedness or emergency management, however, several areas that used to be clearly defined as natural, now in fact could also be man-made.

EMERGENCIES AND DISASTERS

There are numerous lists of emergencies and disasters in emergency management literature. Many lists attempt to categorize these events into the standard categories, "natural" and "man-made," while others obviously list only those events they "handle" or "cover" in their service or support. The following list is an attempt to merge all lists into one unit under general umbrella terms. Obviously emergencies and emergency recovery content overlap, and one event does not exclude another. For example, content on "fire" will more than likely include content from "water damage," while treatment for water damage might be a blend between "fire" recovery (even though materials may be burned or smoke-damaged first) and flood recovery information.

General categories for emergencies include:

- Civil disturbances, conflicts, terrorism, and wars
- Earthquakes

- Explosions
- Fires (forest fires, wildfires, and building/grounds fires)
- Hazardous materials (chemical spills/accidents, human elements, nuclear accidents, oil spills, radiological accidents, and toxic gas releases)
- Landslides
- Mass population displacement/refugee emigration
- Pestilence
- Volcanic activity
- Water (dam and pipe failure, floods, tsunami, and recovery from fire)
- Weather (cyclones, droughts, heat, hurricanes, thunderstorms, tornados, typhoons, and winter storms)
- Workplace violence (bodily harm and trauma)
  - Individuals (staff-generated—vandalism, armed conflict or combat, and threats and attacks including murder)
  - Individuals (non-staff- generated—vandalism, armed conflict or combat, and threats and attacks including murder)

Natural Disasters and Libraries

Natural disasters can affect library buildings; the infrastructure that supports delivery of library resources and services (for example, communications); library constituents; library staff; library partners; and the use of the library for typical transactions as well as the use of resources and services to assist in emergency and disaster response and recovery. Natural disasters can occur within a library only, within the community where the library resides, or can occur in and affect the library's umbrella organization and larger community.

Earthquakes Earthquake activity and the impact of earthquakes or earthquake activity exists in many locations around the world. In some locations, residents experience major impacts that affect buildings, building infrastructures, and transportation structures, while other locations experience more subtle changes connected to library resources or changes to building infrastructures that show more visual devastation. Libraries, housed in a wide variety of buildings and locations, are obviously not immune from damage and destruction and are not guaranteed to survive given the assortment of physical locations. Due to the expenses of repairs and recovery, libraries must focus on assessing risks prior to activities, such as identifying potential issues for resources and services, obtaining insurance with reasonable deductibles, and organizing repair and recovery processes.

Fires (Forest Fires, Wildfire, Buildings/Grounds Fires)   Obviously fires can be natural disasters or man-made disasters. The effects of fire in libraries can include: major destruction of buildings; destruction of collections; repair and recovery of furniture; repair and recovery of hardware and software; and conservation of collections with diverse formats and resources that have smoke, fire, or water damage. These types of damage can occur when environments suffer full-blown fires or when environments suffer smoke damage and non fire-related damage (for example, burned out ballasts and lighting) as well as from water recovery. Related damage may take place in water-logged materials in the form of mold, mildew, and related pestilence. Although all damage is critical, fire and smoke damage has so *many* overlapping elements, it is often considered the most difficult emergency for recovery.

Landslides   Although landslides are not an everyday occurrence, and one would think they typically occur only in certain environments, they can happen in a much broader variety of locations, given climate and weather variations, including extreme heat and lack of moisture; as ice and thawing; building and development use, design, and placement of earth and soil; erosion; and other natural disasters, such as earthquakes. Landslides can invade libraries and ruin building infrastructure and related infrastructure, including transportation and communications. Repair and recovery, insurance, water conservation, and mud damage overlap (as with so many other emergencies and disasters) when identifying and drawing attention to these problems.

Pestilence   Pestilence is typically used to identify widespread contagious or epidemic disease; however, pestilence is also used to describe a destructive parasite that could include insect infestation as well as mold or mildew infecting an environment or resources within the environment. Libraries often have pestilence infesting resources and buildings that can be caused by building conditions that may or may not be caused by other emergency or disaster conditions. Library books and other library resources, such as media or realia, may be infested with insects, mold, or mildew, and these might be introduced through constituent care (or lack thereof) of resources as well as water from the environment including water introduced for fire recovery.

Volcanic Activity   Although this emergency/disaster is least experienced by the general population and libraries, clearly destruction from this activity might be fire (either direct or indirect), heat, smoke damage, or water damage repair and recovery. Many volcanic disturbances are coupled or overlap with earthquakes or earthquake conditions; therefore, as with other disasters, recovery might overlap and could include infrastructure destruction, fire, smoke, heat, and water recovery.

Water (Dam and Pipe Failure, Floods, Tsunami, and Recovery from Fire)   Water is the great element involved in recovery; it is also a destructive force. Given this dichotomy, water—no matter where it comes from—both hurts and heals. Rain water and natural water are treated differently (and the resources affected by them) than water that comes from the ground and is filtered through other environments. Other factors include the amount of water; the length of time water is present; the temperature of the air/water throughout the duration of the emergency; disaster and recovery; and the resources affected (including the type of paper, the age of the resources, resource packaging, the age of packing, any other packing materials); and the nature of emergency and disaster. However, the presence of some water signals complete devastation with no hope for resource or building recovery (major floods, no matter the cause), while other water provides a variety of avenues for partial or complete recovery.

Weather (Cyclones, Droughts, Heat, Hurricanes, Thunderstorms, Tornados, Typhoons, and Winter Storms) Weather, never easy to predict, is considered a major issue in primary emergency and disaster recovery and management in the twenty-first century. Administrators and managers find it hard to prepare for expected weather, much less unexpected weather conditions including unusual heat; thaws related to heat; erosion related to climate change; dust and wind conditions; "body of water" and "body of water to land" emergencies and disasters, such as hurricanes, tornados, typhoons, and thunderstorms. Unusual weather also includes snow and the damage it causes. Obviously the weather and climate (water, heat, wind, and so on) can have an enormous effect on buildings and resources as well as recovery processes. While administrators and managers understandably tend to focus on major emergencies and disasters and recovering from them, attention should be also paid to facilities that lack proper climate control, "creeping problems," spiking hot and cold temperatures, costs, and so on. These conditions can cause pestilence problems, destruction of all types of resources, and also destroy building infrastructure because of expanding and shrinking soil and building elements.

Nonnatural Disasters and Libraries

Civil Disturbances, Conflicts, Terrorism, and Wars Library and information environments, as all other institutions, are affected by the political and social forces that surround them. Although many libraries throughout the United States might not be directly affected by civil disturbances, conflicts, terrorism, and wars, as we move into the twenty-first century we see increasing activity in these areas, and the likelihood of the staff or their families being affected by these events is great. These events also affect publishing and access to print information as well as information available on the web.

It should also be noted that libraries throughout the world may be directly affected by emergencies and disasters, including being bombed or burned during conflicts and being looted. Clearly the loss of both general and unique content and resources affects access to information needed by the global market. An additional impact of disturbances, conflicts, terrorism, and wars is enacted public policy that affects access to and availability of information.

Explosions Explosions may be caused by man-made events either deliberately (terrorism and vandalism) or accidentally; however, weather may also cause explosions and the ensuing damage might include fire and/or water damage. In addition, if explosions are caused by hazardous materials (see the following), then library building and resource recovery from substances will necessitate unique cleaning.

Hazardous Materials (Chemical Spills/Accidents, Human Elements, Nuclear Accidents, Oil Spills, Radiological Accidents, Toxic Gas Releases) Unfortunately, hazardous materials not only occur in the environment (nuclear, radiological, and so on) but also are often found in the typical library workplace. This reality may be hard to grasp, but these materials may be individual elements, such as specific cleaning fluids or fuels, or may be the result of the combination of specific elements. In addition, contemporary equipment or its elements such as those found in batteries and cartridges may be dangerous. Along with natural and man-made elements, hazardous materials may also include human blood and other human fluids. Although not all hazardous materials need cleanup by HazMat (Hazardous Materials) standards, all handling, disposal, and cleanup must be carefully orchestrated. Hazardous effects may also include the unseen effects of hardware and equipment monitor displays or emanations (from wireless frequencies and security gates) on staff and constituents. This also includes not only a specific piece of hardware or equipment, in and of itself, but also the placement or proximity of resources to other hardware, equipment, or to construction elements like steel.

While prevention is not always a possibility in other emergency and disaster issues, it is a major element of emergency management regarding hazardous materials. These materials should be kept separate, the materials contained within equipment and hardware should be limited and carefully managed for use, and the replacement and removal of said equipment, as well as the placement and proximity of the equipment should be addressed

Mass Population Displacement/Refugee Emigration Libraries, although not officially the first responders, play a major role in supporting a community as it experiences changes in population. Population displacement and emigration dictate expanded resources and services, which mean increased funding and expanded expertise. The nature of assisting in assimilating individuals into communities also directly relates to whether or not these individuals are displaced by emergencies and disasters in other communities or by political or social events.

Workplace Violence (Bodily Harm and Trauma)

Individuals (Staff-Generated—Vandalism, Armed Conflict/Combat, and Threats and Attacks, Including Murder) Organizations are not immune to staff-caused emergencies and disasters due to mental instability and illness, or excessive anger. Although libraries have not had many staff behavior disasters like the post office and private sector have, it is possible that library staff can cause destruction to the building, resources, and data as well as to their peers or those in administration and management.

Individuals (Non-staff-Generated Include Vandalism, Armed Conflict or Combat, and Threats and Attacks Including Murder) Library constituents and individuals in umbrella organizations (for example, school campus or city facility settings) as well as those wishing to make "public statements" in any public buildings may cause vandalism, cause conflict (including armed conflict), and make threats. In addition, the library may be the target because a non-staff member may have a problem with a staff member or a family member who is a library staff member.

RESPONSES TO EMERGENCIES AND DISASTERS: TODAY

Responses to emergencies and disasters are dramatically different in today's library and information settings; and running these organizations is more difficult because of increased communication technology for notifying and handling emergencies, the seriousness of some conflicts, the range and variety of emergencies, and the breadth of some destruction (deaths of individuals, data destruction, and so on). Unfortunately, today's managers are not familiar with emergency and disaster management; therefore, they are not equipped to prevent or handle situations as they arise. While today's libraries have addressed some emergencies and disasters through policies, procedures, and disaster planning, not all emergency management elements are in place.

RESPONSES TO EMERGENCIES AND DISASTERS: TOMORROW/FUTURE

Administrators and managers, not equipped to handle many emergencies and disasters today, are ill-equipped for future emergencies and disasters. While managers try to catch up to today's responsibilities, they must not only be learning about tomorrow's issues for equipment/hardware, hazardous materials, inclement weather, and conflict (to name but a few areas), but must also be integrating extensive continuing education and training for staff; implementing plans for issue awareness and budgetary needs for boards and umbrella organization administrations; and grasping risk factors for organizations, including the value and assets of the organization. Tomorrow's organizations need extensive articulated written plans as well as significant funds and structures in place to protect staff, constituents, and real estate.

TWENTY-FIRST CENTURY INFRASTRUCTURE: ORGANIZATIONS, ASSOCIATIONS, AND COMMERCIAL/VENDOR

There are many existing organizations and associations are in place to assist administrators and managers address the needs of the organization. These entities include long-standing resources that have expanded to include contemporary situations, newly formed groups to support new situations, and entities to divide content between home concerns and workplace concerns. The private/vendor/commercial sector has grown at an enormous rate, and great variety exists for acquiring resources to assist in emergency management. (See "Appendices" for an annotated list of resources including organizations, associations, and commercial/vendors.)

TWENTY-FIRST CENTURY PUBLICATIONS: PERIODICALS, MONOGRAPHS, AND THE ONLINE ENVIRONMENT

Just as entities have increased in great numbers, emergency management publishing has grown in both popular and scholarly content in a number of formats, including existing journals, new journals dedicated to emergency management, and monographs on the topic. The emergency management field is developing and although there are significant publications in this area, there are also a growing number of emergency management resources within library and information science publications dealing just with buildings and resources in all types of library and information settings.

The online environment provides extensive resources for administrators and managers in *general* emergency management content. Resources specific to types of libraries are present on the Web primarily in academic libraries with some available for public libraries. Resources by type of library, however, are typically those documents created just for those organizations rather than designated best practice or benchmark resources. (See "Appendices" for an annotated list of resources of periodicals, monographs, and online content.)

TWENTY-FIRST CENTURY TRAINING, CONTINUING EDUCATION, AND PROFESSIONAL DEVELOPMENT

Although training and continuing education are considered critical components of preparation for, prevention of, and handling of emergency and disaster issues, and although there is much general education on emergency management, this general education is very expensive. In addition, no extensive emergency management training exists for the library and information science profession—much less for specific types of libraries. In addition, the curriculum of professional, graduate, and continuing education in library and information science is not extensive. (See "Appendices" for an annotated list of resources of training, continuing education, and professional development.)

TWENTY-FIRST CENTURY DOCUMENTS: FORMS/CHECKLISTS

Strategic plans, forms, checklists, and related materials are the mainstay of emergency management content and professional literature. Even though the existing content is more general than specific to the library and information science field, existing documents and forms and checklists are easily converted to preparation and assessment of library and information settings. Administrators and managers of all types of library settings can use umbrella organization content as well as general "government issued" content. (See "Appendices" for an annotated list of resources of general documents as well as recommendations for template forms and checklists.)

2

DEFINING TWENTY-FIRST CENTURY EMERGENCIES AND DISASTERS IN LIBRARY ENVIRONMENTS

CONTENTS

- Scenario: Natural
- Scenario: Man-made
- Unique Aspects of Library Settings
- Library Umbrella Organizations
- External Emergencies and Disasters/Library Environments
- Internal Emergencies and Disasters/Library Environments

DEFINING TWENTY-FIRST CENTURY EMERGENCIES AND DISASTERS IN LIBRARY ENVIRONMENTS

Learning how to deal with emergencies in general is a complex process, and learning how to deal with emergencies and how they apply to library environments (academic, school, public, and special libraries) is even more complex. Although there is much talk in the literature about the worst emergencies and disasters and although libraries have been involved in and affected by them (9/11, Katrina, and so on), the majority are just as "real," but thankfully not catastrophic. In the literature, the types of situations and events that typically occur include:

- Theft of property/library materials
- Vandalism /mutilation of library materials
- Computer vandalism and /or data destruction
- Inappropriate, illegal area activities (unique areas, such as small group rooms and restrooms)
- Vandalism /destructive activities of facilities /resources
- Safety for staff and constituents (hazardous materials, such as chemicals and molds)
- Fire, smoke, and ensuing water damage
- Water damage from flooding and leaks

- Constituent behavior
- Pestilence

Deciding where to look and how to frame the questions is difficult as well. One can find content to assist in dealing with situations and events under the following headings: life saving; natural disasters; fire/smoke; chemical hazards and hazardous waste; human fluids; office safety or occupational safety information; ergonomics or occupational safety information; incident management; accommodation (relating to safety) and emergency management; emergency preparedness; and disaster planning.

No matter where you look or what you call it, using scenarios (often used synonymously with case method process) to frame situations and events provides administrators and managers not only with answers but also with a process to replicate when faced with their own situations.

Scenarios throughout the monograph are set in a variety of types of libraries. These two scenarios, representing a natural emergency and a man-made emergency, are set in public library environments. Immediately following each of these scenarios is the scenario issue and problem-solving process applied to and worked through each case.

The four sections following these two cases provide unique elements and characteristics of each type of library. This information provides the "definition" of twenty-first century emergencies and disasters within each type of library environment.

SCENARIO: NATURAL

The weather forecast for the city had been predicting rain and storms for some time. Following a lack of any precipitation since midspring, community members were concerned about a strong weather front creating conditions where water might accumulate and cause flooding.

Wainsborough Public Library, faced with an active summer reading club schedule of activities for children and teens, decided to continue programming for the weekend in the absence of a formal "emergency conditions" prediction by weather/newscasters and city management. The youth and young adult library staff continued with preparations for the teen read-in for Friday night but decided to keep an eye on the weather.

Friday morning began as overcast, and by noon the sky was gray but not ominous. While staff kept an eye on the weather, plans for the read-in went ahead and by 4:00 p.m., the library was filled with young people and the favorite three books they wanted to share with others. At 7:00 p.m., however, the rain began—not with a drizzle—but with a major downpour. By 8:30, the streets and the sidewalks were filled with water, and the library's parking lot was flooded with over twelve inches of water.

Library phones and teen cell phones began to ring as parents called to check on their children and to say that official statements from city management indicated that everyone should stay off the streets. A few parents made it to the library but then couldn't easily leave as the intersection near the library was completed flooded. By 9:15 p.m., police had set up roadblocks, and no cars were allowed in or out of the intersection, which meant the library parking lot was inaccessible.

Library staff members were faced with an evening—possibly a sleepover—with dozens of teens! In addition, the library's rear staff door opened onto the parking lot at lot level and as the front of the lot filled, water began to seep into the staff entrance area.

Steps to Solutions

1. Read the case and study the situation thoroughly. Take no immediate position or role. Underline what you feel are the impor-

tant or relevant facts or statements. Some suggested points have
been italicized below.

The weather forecast for the city had been *predicting rain and storms
for some time*. Following a lack of any precipitation since midspring,
community members were concerned about a strong weather front
creating conditions where water might accumulate and *cause flooding*.

Wainsborough Public Library, faced with an active summer reading club schedule of activities for children and teens, *decided to continue programming* for the weekend *in the absence of a formal
"emergency conditions" prediction* by weather/newscasters and city
management. The youth' and young adult library staff continued with
preparations for the teen read-in for Friday night but decided to *keep
an eye on the weather*.

Friday morning began as overcast, and by noon the sky was gray
but not ominous. While staff *kept an eye on the weather*, plans for the
read-in went ahead and by 4 p.m., the library was filled with young
people and the favorite three books they wanted to share with others. At 7:00 p.m., however, the rain began—not with a drizzle—but
with a major downpour. By 8:30, the streets and the sidewalks were
filled with water, and the library's parking lot was flooded with over
twelve inches of water.

Library phones and teen cell phones began to ring as parents
called to check on their children and *to say that official statements from
city management indicated that everyone should stay off the streets*. A
few parents made it to the library but then couldn't easily leave as
the intersection near the library was completed flooded. By 9:15
p.m., police had set up roadblocks, and *no cars were allowed in or out
of the intersection, which meant the library parking lot was inaccessible*.

Library staff members were faced with an evening—possibly a
sleepover—with dozens of teens! In addition, the library's rear staff
door opened onto the parking lot at lot level and as the front of the
lot filled, *water began to seep into the staff entrance area*.

2. List the important or relevant facts or statements of the situation.

- This was not an immediate or unexpected event. Rain, storms, and flooding had been predicted.
- The library made a conscious decision to continue its activities.
- Library managers were waiting for an official emergency notification from the city.
- Library staff members were attempting to monitor the weather.
- Library staff members did not address the rain situation when it began even though the rain began as a downpour and water accumulation occurred immediately.
- Parents expressed concern immediately, and several parents were at the library as well as teens.
- The city administration made an official ruling later in the evening.
- City workers (under direction from city officials) set up roadblocks that shut off access to and from the library.
- Library staff members were faced with an evening of constituents staying overnight at a public facility.
- Library staff members are faced with possible flooding of the library.

3. List the characters or "players" in the situation, and list them in relevant categories. Several categories might be: those directly involved, those indirectly involved, and those affected by the situation.

Staff in the library serving constituents during this situation

- Staff in the library during this situation and managing this event/these constituents

- Constituents in the library mentioned in the case
- Constituents in the library not mentioned in the case but possibly using the library in activities not connected to this event
- Teens in the library program
- Parents who came to the library when concerned
- Parents phoning teens to find out what was going on

Indirectly Involved:

- Administration/management of the library other than those previously listed
- Parents who did not go to the library
- Parents who did not phone
- Parents expecting to pick up teens when the program is over
- Individuals responsible for handling building repairs
- Individuals responsible for assessing flooding conditions and closing/opening up the library

Others Affected by the Situation:

- Constituents wanting to use the library but finding it closed
- Library staff coming to work for evening shifts

4. List the primary issues or problems in the situation.

- Safety issues concerning the public spending the night in a city facility
- Safety issues concerning underage teens spending the night in a city facility
- Flooding in the library—damaging resources
- Communication issues on library closure because parents need to know about their children
- Coordinating constituents exiting the library under post-flood conditions

5. Given what you know, prioritize the issues or problems in the situation.

- Flooding in the library—damaging resources
- Safety issues concerning underage teens spending the night in a city facility
- Safety issues concerning the public spending the night in a city facility
- Communication issues on library closure because parents need to know about their children
- Coordinating constituents exiting the library under post-flood conditions

6. After reviewing the situation, list "what can be done" or possible solutions for each issue or problem. Some suggestions are listed in tables 2.1 and 2.2 below.

Table 2.1

Situation Statements	Should Have Done
This was not an immediate or unexpected event. Rain, storms, and flooding had been predicted.	Staff members should have discussed canceling the event following discussions with city management; if available, city risk management. In addition, a backup plan should have been discussed or designed.
The library made a conscious decision to continue its activities.	A backup plan should have been in place.
Library managers were waiting for an official emergency notification from the city.	Although this might have been a more formal process, it seems casual. There should be a communication chain or plan from the city-to-city facilities, and there should be a plan for communicating emergency situations among library staff.
Library staff members were attempting to monitor the weather.	City facilities should all have National Oceanic and Atmospheric Administration (NOAA) weather radio, which staff should

Table 2.1 (Continued)

	monitor. In addition, many facilities offer two-way radio communication between city facilities and city law enforcement.
Library staff members did not address the rain situation when it began, even though the rain began as a downpour and water accumulation occurred immediately.	A backup plan should have been in place and should "kick in" when rain becomes an issue.
Parents expressed concern immediately, and several parents were at the library with the teens.	Staff should have had preprinted signs on the library front doors announcing alternative plans as well as handouts for parents to provide information should a weather emergency occur.
City administration made an official ruling later in the evening.	Staff should be monitoring the communication plan process that alerts city facilities that city management has made a decision.
City workers (under directions from city officials) set up roadblocks that shut off access or exit from the library.	Staff should be working with maintenance to determine flood conditions and road closures.
Library staff members were faced with an evening of constituents staying overnight at a public facility.	Library staff should have a plan of action ready for "shelter in place" plans that typically organize response and handling for up to 72 hours. Library resources should include emergency kits and "shelter in place" materials for housing, protecting, and feeding those involved in emergency activities.
Library staff members were faced with possible flooding of the library.	Staff should have a plan for shoring up excessive water, including materials to stop water (sandbags) as well as clean up water. Additional flood support resources should include plans for relocating materials near the flooded area and protective clothing for staff that need to clean up/stop water prior to city support services arriving at the library. City personnel who take care of water issues should be part of the library's emergency communication plan and should be available through two-way radio systems.

Table 2.2

Elements of the Situation	What Can Be Done
Flooding in the library—damaging resources	Library administration and management should have an emergency preparedness plan that includes water and facility issues. This plan should include preliminary actions for dealing with excessive water, including resources to stop water (sandbags) as well as eliminating water until experts arrive. Emergency preparedness plans also include a communication plan that covers requesting expert staff and then communicating with expert staff during the event. Additional flood support resources should include plans for relocating materials in or near the flooded area and protective clothing for staff that need to clean up/stop water prior to city support services arriving at the library. Plans should also include recovery of facilities as well as recovery of materials and resources damaged in the event. Plans should be accompanied by kits or sets of resources to assist in the event.
Safety issues concerning underage teens spending the night in a city facility	Library staff should have a plan of action ready for "shelter in place" plans that typically organizes response and handling for up to 72 hours. This plan should have sections for adult "shelter in place" as well as for underage constituents. Library resources should include emergency kits and "shelter in place" materials for housing, protecting, and feeding those involved in emergency activities. Although staff must adhere to Health Insurance Portability and Accountability Act (HIPAA) guidelines, care must taken to assess any unique health issues and needs of those staying in the library.

Table 2.2 (Continued)

Safety issues concerning the public spending the night in a city facility	Library staff should have a plan of action ready for "shelter in place" plans that typically organize response and handling for up to 72 hours. Library resources should include emergency kits and "shelter in place" materials for housing, protecting, and feeding those involved in emergency activities. Staff should work with teen parents to organize activities, seek support, and establish guidelines for "sheltering in place." Although staff must adhere to HIPAA guidelines, care must taken to assess any unique health issues and needs of those staying in the library.
Communication issues on library closure because parents need to know about their children	If possible, the city should have emergency notification on television and radio channels. While staff monitor those and NOAA weather radio, staff should have a series of preprinted signs posted on the library front doors announcing closure and plans for those staying in the library overnight. Standardized messages on library phones should be utilized; scripts for what to tell parents when they call should be available for those set up to answer phones. Teens and parents of teens in the library should be given handouts with standardized information to tell parents when they call. Handouts for individuals in the library should be available with information on sleeping, eating, and safety guidelines as well as guidelines for behavior until the event is over. A phone and e-mail chain (if all resources are working) should be established for informing staff of event issues as well as a phone tree to inform city administration of the situation. Rescue/responders in the area, such as community police and fire fighters, should be notified of alternative uses of city facilities.

Coordinating constituents exiting the library under post-flood conditions	Staff designated in charge of the event should inventory those in the library and keep a running tally of who is in the library and who is leaving and when they leave. In addition, library managers should coordinate the use of "shelter in place" kits.

7. List what can't be done, given any limitations or relevant facts. Match what can't be done with the relevant issues as needed. Some suggestions are listed in table 2.3 below:

Table 2.3

Elements of the Situation	What Can't Be Done
Flooding in the library—damaging resources	Staff cannot ignore the flooding nor choose to only handle themselves and not notify city support services. Staff cannot choose to ignore resources affected by water.
Safety issues concerning underage teens spending the night in a city facility	Staff should not allow anyone other than staff to take charge. Staff should not, if at all possible, allow any teens to leave the library unattended/with their parent or guardian.
Safety issues concerning the public spending the night in a city facility	Staff should not allow anyone other than staff to take charge of the situation. Staff should not allow adults to remove teens without permission of the teens' parents.
Communication issues on library closure because parents need to know about their children	Staff should not communicate everything verbally and have no written instructions/guidelines. Staff, if at all possible, should speak with parents who call rather than only letting teens communicate what is happening. Staff should gather phone numbers and follow up with phone calls post-event to see if everyone is "okay."
Coordinating constituents exiting the library under postflood conditions	Staff should not let individuals leave without an inventory of who was there and when they left as well as gathering e-mails, home addresses, and phone numbers.

8. Choose the best one or two solutions, matching up any solutions with what can't be done.

Although how the situation is handled is relatively clear-cut and simple, the two most important things to be aware of and to handle include the flooding of the library even though it appears to be minor AND that the library staff must take charge of the underage constituent situation. Some suggestions are listed in table 2.4 below.

Table 2.4

Situations	Solutions
Flooding in the library—damaging resources	Staff cannot ignore the flooding nor choose to only handle themselves and not notify city support services. Staff cannot choose to ignore resources affected by water.
Safety issues concerning underage teens spending the night in a city facility	Staff should not allow anyone other than staff to take charge. Staff should not, if at all possible, allow any teens to leave the library unattended/without their parent or guardian.

9. Speculate on the outcome if the solutions are put into effect. Some suggestions are listed in table 2.5 below:

Table 2.5

Elements of the Situation	What Can Be Done	Possible Outcomes
Flooding in the library/damaging resources	Library administration and management should have an emergency preparedness plan that includes water and facility issues. This plan should include preliminary actions for dealing with excessive water, including resources to stop water (sandbags) as well as eliminating water until experts arrive. Emergency preparedness plans should also include a communication plan that covers requesting expert staff and then communicating with	Staff participating in the recovery should be protected. Water should be stopped before much damage is done to the facility. Facility flooring, etc. should be recovered. Damage to resources should be minimal, and wet resources should be recovered and restored.

	expert staff during the event. Additional flood support resources should include plans for relocating materials in or near the flooded area and protective clothing for staff that need to clean up/stop water prior to city support services arriving at the library. Plans should also include recovery of facilities as well as recovery of materials and resources damaged in the event. Plans should be accompanied by kits or sets of resources to assist in the event.	
Safety issues concerning underage teens spending the night in a city facility	Library staff should have a plan of action ready for "shelter in place" plans that typically organize response and handling for up to 72 hours. This plan should have sections for adult "shelter in place" as well as for underage constituents. Library resources should include emergency kits and "shelter in place" materials for housing, protecting, and feeding those involved in emergency activities. Although staff must adhere to HIPAA guidelines, care must be taken to assess any unique health issues and needs of those staying in the library.	For the length of the event, teens should be safe, and there should be minimum conflict or acting out. All individuals having to stay at the library for the length of the event should have adequate supplies and resources. All teens should leave with few health issues, and if any, none should be related to the library event. Teens should leave with good feelings about their stay in the library. Parents should have no complaints on how teens were treated or how the event was handled and that the event was well managed.

Table 2.5 (Continued)

Safety issues concerning the public spending the night in a city facility	Library staff should have a plan of action ready for "shelter in place" plans that typically organize response and handling for up to 72 hours. Library resources should include emergency kits and "shelter in place" materials for housing, protecting, and feeding those involved in emergency activities. Staff should work with teen parents to organize activities, seek support, and establish guidelines for "sheltering in place." Although staff must adhere to HIPAA guidelines, care must betaken to assess any unique health issues and needs of those staying in the library.	Any constituents staying through the event should feel the event was well managed. All constituents should leave with few health issues and, if any, none should be related to the library event. All individuals having to stay at the library for the length of the event should have adequate supplies and resources. Library staff should make good decisions based on the information available to them.
Communication issues on library closure because parents need to know about their children	If possible, the city should have emergency notification on television and radio channels. While staff monitor those and NOAA weather radio, staff should have a series of preprinted signs posted and on the library front doors announcing closure and plans for those in the library overnight. Standardized messages on library phones should be utilized, and scripts for what to tell parents when they call should be available for those set up to answer phones. Teens and parents of teens in the library should be given handouts with standardized information to tell parents when they call. Handouts for individuals in the library should be available with information on sleeping, eating, and safety guidelines as well as guidelines for behavior until the event is over. A phone and e-mail chain (if all resources are working) should be established for informing staff of event issues as well as a phone tree to	Communication throughout the event should have been clear and consistent and have come from multiple official sources. Individuals needing information should have received the information they needed in a timely fashion. Parents should have felt they had access to up-to-date, accurate information.

	inform city administration of the situation. Rescue/responders in the area, such as community police and firefighters, should be notified of alternative uses of city facilities.	
Coordinating constituents exiting the library under post-flood conditions	Staff designated as in charge of the event should inventory those in the library and keep a running tally of who is in the library and who is leaving and when they leave. In addition, library managers should coordinate the use of "shelter in place" kits.	Constituents should have left the library feeling they were treated well, were safe, and that the library staff managed the situation appropriately. Constituents should feel good about the library following the event.

10. Build in an evaluation mechanism.

- Library administrators and managers design a postevent meeting with all staff involved.
- The library's emergency preparedness plan is assessed to determine if it covered all that was needed for the event, if it provided the appropriate scripts, and if available signage was adequate.
- Library staff contact constituents involved in the event to assess their opinions about how the event was handled.
- Library staff conduct an inventory of emergency kits to determine if resources were appropriate and plentiful.
- Resources recovered from the flood are assessed by a conservator to determine if the resources can be introduced back in to the collection.
- Library staff follow up with city personnel to determine why the staff door flooded and request that they be given a plan for redesign of the area to avoid future flooding.

11. Consider the need to have both short-range and long-range solutions.

- Short-range solutions for improving handling of the event might include staff training of how they handled constituents, scripts used for answering the phone/dealing with parents, and replacement of any kit materials used during the event.
- Long-range solutions might be rewriting emergency preparedness plans and/or requesting the umbrella institution to come up with standardized processes.

One might delegate all or part of an issue or problem or they might assign timelines (and this might create changes in the process).

- Rewriting, revising or updating plans might include delegating assessment and rewriting of scripts; for example, to an emergency preparedness/disaster planning work group.

SCENARIO: MAN-MADE

Scotland Public Library closed at 2:00 p.m. on Saturdays in the summer months. There were a number of constituents who frequented Saturday hours and, although a number of individuals expressed an interest in extending summer Saturday hours, funding was not available.

A staff member made the rounds at 1:45 announcing the library's closing, but one library user did not acknowledge that the announcement had been made and kept his head down working in his notebook. When the staff member made the second round of announcements, the library user, identifying himself as Ben, challenged library staff by saying that he was not through with his work and that he needed to stay. He loudly expressed displeasure at being asked to leave and made no attempt to gather up his materials. Staff did not respond to the individual's tirade and withdrew from that portion of the library. Staff then caucused behind the circulation desk and decided to make sure that all other constituents were gone from the library and that they needed to call the community police station down the street for assistance. Police responded quickly and asked staff to meet them at the door. Upon arriving at the library and meeting with staff to be briefed on the situation, police then approached the library user, who stood up and began to shout and charge toward police.

After subduing the constituent, police cuffed him and escorted him to their vehicle. While the individual sat in the police car, library staff on duty clarified the paperwork they needed to complete. Police urged the staff to file a complaint against the individual. The manager on duty stated that he would have to contact his manager and library administration to determine how they needed to follow up with police, with the individual, and with library administration.

Steps to Solutions

1. Read the case and study the situation thoroughly. Take no immediate position or role. Underline what you feel are the important or relevant facts or statements. Some suggested points have been italicized below.

Scotland Public Library closed at 2:00 p.m. on Saturdays in the summer months. There were a number of constituents who frequented Saturday hours and, although a number of individuals *expressed an interest in extending summer Saturday hours*, funding was not available.

A staff member made the *rounds at 1:45* announcing the library's closing, but one library user *did not acknowledge that the announcement* had been made and kept his head down working in his notebook. When the *staff member made the second round* of announcements, the library user, identifying himself as Ben, challenged library staff by saying that he was not through with his work and that he needed to stay. He loudly expressed displeasure at being asked to leave and made no attempt to gather up his materials. *Staff did not respond to the individual's tirade* and withdrew from that portion of the library.

Staff then caucused behind the circulation desk and decided to *make sure that all other constituents were gone from the library* and that they needed to call the community police station down the street for assistance. *Police responded quickly and asked staff to meet them at the door.* Upon arriving at the library and meeting with staff to be briefed on the situation, police then approached the library user, who stood up and began to shout and charge toward police.

After subduing the constituent, police cuffed him and escorted him to their vehicle. While the individual sat in the police car, *library staff on duty clarified the paperwork they needed to complete. Police urged the staff to file a complaint* against the individual. The manager on duty stated that he would have to *contact his manager and library administration to determine how they needed to follow up with police, with the individual, and with library administration.*

2. List the important or relevant facts or statements of the situation.

- The library closed early during some months of the year.
- Some constituents had complained about the library closing at 2:00 p.m.
- One staff member made the rounds to close up.
- Staff circulated around the library at fifteen minutes to closing.
- Staff did not address the constituent's comment that he was not through with his work.
- Staff withdrew when the user expressed anger.
- Staff cleared out all other constituents from the library.
- Staff worked with police to brief them of the situation.
- Staff were not sure which paperwork to complete and what the next actions should be.

3. List the characters or "players" in the situation, and list them in relevant categories. Several categories might be: those directly involved, and those affected by the situation.

Directly Involved:

- The library user
- The staff member who had direct contact with the library user
- Other staff in the library at the time of event
- Other library users in the library at closing
- Law enforcement who responded

Indirectly Involved:

- Other library staff who work at the library but aren't on duty
- Library administration and management to make the decision regarding charges
- Those affected by the situation
- Library users on Saturday afternoons
- All staff at the library

4. List the primary issues or problems in the situation.

- Staff did not know a number of techniques to handle library user conflicts.
- Staff did not know how protocols for police/constituent are to be handled.
- Follow-up discussions need to take place among staff to determine how things might better be handled.

5. Given what you know, prioritize the issues or problems in the situation.

- Follow-up discussions need to take place among staff to determine how things might better be handled.
- Staff need training for techniques to handle library user conflicts.

- Staff need training on establishing protocols for police/constituent situations.

6. After reviewing the situation, list "what can be done" or possible solutions for each issue or problem. Some suggested points are listed in table 2.6 below.

Table 2.6

Situations	What Can Be Done
Follow up discussions need to take place among staff to determine how things might better be handled.	Staff members should write individual reports on the event, management should study reports and assess what happened, and then a meeting should be held to identify what worked, what didn't work, what needs to be changed, and who needs to be trained for enhanced or different responses. Documents available (for example, emergency plan) should be compared to facts of event. Library management should also seek feedback from police force.
Staff need training for techniques to handle library user conflicts.	Following assessment, all staff using role play techniques should have training on potentially dangerous situations for staff and constituents.
Staff need training on establishing protocols for police/constituent situations.	Library administration should work with city management to determine follow-up with individuals who breach city and library behavior/facilities guidelines and policies. Incident management information should then be built in to training.

7. List what can't be done, given any limitations or relevant facts. Match what can't be done with the relevant issues as needed. Some suggested points are listed in table 2.7 below.

Table 2.7

Situations	What Can't Be Done
Follow-up discussions need to take place among staff to determine how things might better be handled.	Staff cannot ignore the incident, and they cannot just work with staff who were present during the incident.
	Staff cannot ignore the specific constituent. The likelihood is great that the constituent will return. Administration and management must immediately follow up to determine what is going to happen to that specific individual. For example—booked? Released from jail? Barred from city facilities? Treatment recommended? Required? How will staff handle if constituent returns?
	Training should specifically address how this situation could have been handled differently for this situation and in general including:
	• Staff could begin "closing activities" earlier to give patrons more time to complete specific task.
	• Staff could move throughout the library in pairs for closing activities.
	• Staff could leave time for specific follow-up with patrons to determine ways for those who may or may not specifically seek assistance; for example, continue working at home, check out materials, or possibly have home access to resources?
	• Staff could schedule police (or a security force officer) to arrive at library each evening to assist with closing until staff feel secure. Decide if this should be temporary or permanent service.
Staff need training for techniques to handle library user conflicts.	Require training for all staff including positive language, good customer service, conflict resolution, and personal safety at work training.
Staff need training on establishing protocols for police/constituent situations.	Require training for all staff to handle situations with law enforcement officials including behavior and completing paperwork, etc.

8. Choose the best one or two solutions, matching up any solutions with what can't be done. Some suggested points are listed in table 2.8 below.

Table 2.8

Situations	Best Solutions
Follow up discussions need to take place among staff to determine how things might better be handled.	Deal with the specific constituent. The likelihood is great that the constituent will return. Administration and management must immediately follow up to determine what is going to happen to that specific individual. For example—booked? Released from jail? Barred from city facilities? Treatment recommended? Required? How will staff handle if user returns?
	Training should specifically address how this incident could have been handled differently for this situation and in general including:
	• Staff could begin "closing activities" earlier to give patrons more time to complete specific task.
	• Staff could move throughout the library in pairs for closing activities.
	• Staff could leave time for specific follow-up with patrons to determine ways for those who may or may not specifically seek assistance; for example, continue working at home, check out materials, or possibly have home access to resources?
	• Staff could schedule police (or a security force officer) to arrive at library each evening to assist with closing until staff feel secure. Decide if this should be temporary or permanent service.
Staff need training for techniques to handle library user conflicts.	Require training for all staff including positive language, good customer service, conflict resolution, and personal safety at work training.

9. Speculate on the outcome if the solutions are put into effect. Some suggested points are listed in table 2.9 below.

Table 2.9

Situations	Best Solutions	Outcomes
Follow up discussions need to take place among staff to determine how things might better be handled.	Deal with the specific constituent. The likelihood is great that the constituent will return. Administration and management must immediately follow up to determine what is going to happen to that specific individual. For example—booked? Released from jail? Barred from city facilities? Treatment recommended? Required? How will staff handle if user returns? Training should specifically address how this situation could have been handled differently for this situation and in general including: Staff could begin "closing activities" earlier to give patrons more time to complete specific task. • Staff could move throughout the library in pairs for closing activities. • Staff could leave time for specific follow-up with patrons to determine ways for those who may or may not specifically seek assistance; for example, continue working at home, check out materials, or possibly have home access to resources? • Staff could schedule police (or a security force officer) to arrive at library each evening to assist with closing until staff feel secure. Decide if this should be temporary or permanent service.	Staff are safe and feel safe working in the library. Staff feel secure in handling conflict situations.

Table 2.9 (Continued)

Staff need training for techniques to handle library user conflicts.	Require training for all staff including include positive language, good customer service, conflict resolution, and personal safety at work training.	Staff should feel equipped to handle conflict situations in the library.

10. Build in an evaluation mechanism.

- Administration and management assess staff responses to determine if initial situation was handled correctly against the emergency plan.
- Police feedback is requested and assessed to determine if the situation was handled appropriately.
- Staff opinions are assessed to determine if they feel training is appropriate and if they feel safe in the library environment.

11. Consider the need to have both short-range and long-range solutions.

- One short-range solution would be to deal with the specific constituent. The likelihood is great that the constituent will return. Administration and management must immediately follow up to determine what is going to happen to that specific individual. For example—booked? Released from jail? Barred from city facilities? Treatment recommended? Required? How will staff handle if user returns?
  Other short-range solutions might include ensuring that staff feel safe in returning to the library, scheduling a police visit at closing time to assist staff, and identifying staff partners to close the library in pairs, using specific scripts. Managers could also delegate all or part of a short range activity or solution and/or could establish a short range timeline.
- Long-range solutions may include the following: delegating all or part of an issue or problem or assigning longer time lines (and this might create changes in the process), identifying city

trainers for staff conflict training, and assessing the budget to request dollars in the next budget year for a police and/or security service to assist at library closing times.

UNIQUE ASPECTS OF LIBRARY SETTINGS

Although there are common elements in emergency and disaster plans and planning for different types of libraries, a number of unique aspects concerning each type of library settings cause managers to design and plan elements differently, establish different time lines, and seek different training.

Academic Libraries

Unique aspects of academic libraries regarding emergency management and disaster planning include the following:

- Many academic environments and their umbrella institutions are highly decentralized, and communication among locations is very challenging.
- Previous perceptions of higher education environments convey that they are calm, pastoral settings where constituents are safe. These perceptions often get in the way of creating plans and processes to respond to unsafe events.
- Many higher education *umbrella* institutions have not yet addressed emergency preparedness.
- Guidelines for acceptable and appropriate facilities behavior are often hard to enforce.
- Disaster planning for many academic environments includes complex, multifaceted planning for wide varieties of special collections.
- Many academic environments have their own police force or

security detail. This is beneficial for departments and functions because it signals a better informed and/or more available safety force. The same police force or security detail may
not necessarily be beneficial for libraries as it provides more
levels of staff to go through to get issues/events handled.
- Fewer staff at smaller locations is often a safety and security
  issue.

Public Libraries

Unique aspects of public libraries regarding emergency management and disaster planning include the following:

- Many public libraries are not funded for their own police or
  security force; therefore, systems have little or no security
  and/or protection at branch libraries.
- Infrastructure problems in city and county buildings are often
  apparent due to poor funding for maintenance. This situation
  exacerbates problems with recovery from natural disasters and
  in some situations might cause disasters (for example, poorly
  maintained roofs may leak or collapse from rain and other inclement weather).
- Fewer staff at smaller locations is a safety and security issue.
- While most cities and counties have addressed emergency issues, most existing plans do not include details relevant to specific resources and services of public libraries.
- Most public libraries are not funded for adequate support of
  emergency preparedness or disaster planning recovery materials.

School Libraries

Unique aspects of school libraries regarding emergency management and disaster planning include the following:

- Individual school libraries do not have individual budgets for support of emergency management and disaster planning, and this lack of funding might prevent managers from buying emergency kits and resources to support health, recovery, and notification.
- Campus-based management processes at school districts allow principals to create their own plans for managing buildings and resources in emergency and disaster situations, but it prohibits libraries from forming cohesive *system-wide library* emergency preparedness and disaster plans.
- Many schools do not have school librarians assigned to full- or part-time work at campuses. This lack of staff means that normal operating activities do not get carried out, much less those activities that would manage emergencies or disaster recovery.

Special Libraries

Unique aspects of special libraries regarding emergency management and disaster planning include the following:

- Umbrella organizations of special libraries vary dramatically and can include nonprofits, not-for-profits, and profit environments. These can include government agencies, business and industry, and the health professions. Because of this variety, identifying benchmarks and best practices is very challenging.
- Many special libraries have proprietary information that cannot be recovered following emergencies or disasters.
- Many special libraries do not have librarians assigned full time or at all. This lack of staff means that normal operating activities do not get carried out much less those activities that would manage emergencies or disaster recovery.

LIBRARY UMBRELLA ORGANIZATIONS

The vast majority of all types of libraries have umbrella organizations. In the last ten years, these umbrella organizations (cities, counties, higher education, school districts, business and industry, etc.) have moved extensively into the assessment of risk factors in emergency and disaster situations as well as aggressively into the identification of primary responsibility for budget funding, and the articulation of emergency and disaster plans and training.

Although these umbrella organizations include all departments and functions in their planning, the reality is that library and information settings and resources have many unique characteristics that need special attention in emergency and disaster planning. These elements include:

- Housing, care, and recovery of resources either not found or not found in such large numbers (books, periodicals, media formats, realia, equipment, and software)
- Data/metadata
- Larger numbers of resources in one location as well as resources spread out (throughout a city, on multiple floors of buildings, etc.)

EXTERNAL EMERGENCIES AND
DISASTERS/LIBRARY ENVIRONMENTS

Given special needs, libraries need to identify and form unique relationships with external emergency and disaster management areas. These include:

- Local entities charged with specific responsibility for handling emergency and disaster events

- Federal entities (for example, FEMA offices affiliated with most counties)
- Umbrella institutional offices designated as responsible for handling emergency and disaster events
- Funding sources (grants from local, state, federal agencies; foundations; philanthropic opportunities; entrepreneurial possibilities)
- Designated community experts for consulting? Training? Recovery?
- Commercial entities for consulting? Training? Recovery?

INTERNAL EMERGENCIES AND DISASTERS/LIBRARY ENVIRONMENTS

Libraries need to establish areas of responsibility for issues related to emergency and disaster planning, implementation, and recovery issues. Activities could be assigned to individuals, small groups, and specific departments and include:

- Training
- Communication with staff
- Communication with umbrella organization entities
  - Local entities charged with specific responsibility for handling emergency and disaster events
  - Federal entities (for example, FEMA offices affiliated with most counties)
  - Umbrella institutional offices designated as responsible for handling emergency and disaster events
  - Funding sources (grants from local, state, federal agencies; foundations; philanthropic opportunities; and entrepreneurial possibilities)
  - Designated community experts
  - Commercial entities

- Communication with constituents
- Budget issues (funding levels; accounts available for buying, hiring resources, and services)
- Housing, care, and recovery of resources (books, periodicals, media formats, realia, equipment, and software)
- Data/metadata on-site and off-site storage and recovery

PLANNING, PREVENTION, RESPONSE, AND RECOVERY

CONTENTS

- Scenario: Planning for All Types of Libraries
- Library Elements in Planning, Prevention, Response, and Recovery

3

PLANNING, PREVENTION, RESPONSE, AND RECOVERY

SCENARIO: PLANNING FOR ALL TYPES OF LIBRARIES

Disaster Plan

Elspeth Monroe had been the library manager for almost eighteen months. A librarian, however, for over twenty years, she had observed a number of events that occurred in and around library and information settings. These events ranged from serious events and activities and included disasters (extensive water in a large urban public library branch, fire and smoke damage in a large academic library, and a hostage situation in a prison library) to emergency events and activities (a planned renovation of a second floor of a special library "host" environment when the ceiling leaked unusual liquid; a constituent having a heart attack in the library).

When she first took over management of her library, she inventoried the "files" and found that although library policies in most areas seemed to be current, some procedures were not and, most importantly for her, the library had few policies and no written plans and little discussion on what would happen should their older seventh-floor library environment be affected by or involved in an emergency situation or a disaster. Given this observation and the lack of written information, Elspeth immediately purchased a medical kit and identified staff to assist her in creating an initial plan of action should something occur. In addition, she identified similar library settings to hers and requested copies of their emergency documents and received permission to use content from two websites that provided basic information. Asking her staff to assist her in selecting the best information or most relevant content from other libraries and web materials in the first six months of her management, Elspeth created a quick set of crucial policies and procedures. These addressed protection of her staff and constituents, brought in local emergency and first responder individuals in the community to provide a half-day workshop for staff, and asked the appropriate individuals to assess and recommend building signage regarding emergency management issues.

Elspeth had noted at her one-year anniversary with the organization that she needed to return to the emergency and disaster issues in earnest, identify dollars and bring together a team, and prepare a full-scale disaster plan and emergency management policies and procedures. Now, eighteen months into her tenure as manager, her work group was well underway to creating the appropriate "disaster and emergency management plan" for the library.

Steps to Solutions

1. Read the case, study the situation thoroughly. Take no immediate position or role. Underline what you feel are the important or relevant facts or statements.

Elspeth Monroe had been the library manager for almost eighteen months. A librarian, however, for over twenty years, she had observed a number of events that occurred in and around library and information settings. These events ranged from serious events and activities and included disasters (extensive water in a large urban public library branch, fire and smoke damage in a large academic library, and a hostage situation in a prison library) to emergency events and activities (a planned renovation of a second floor of a spe cial library "host" environment when the ceiling leaked unusual liquid; a constituent having a heart attack in the library).

When she first took over management of her library, she inventoried the "files" and found that although library policies in most areas seemed to be current, some procedures were not and, most importantly for her, the library had few policies and no written plans and little discussion on what would happen should their older seventh-floor library environment be affected by or involved in an emergency situation or a disaster. Given this observation and the lack of written information, Elspeth immediately purchased a medical kit and identified staff to assist her in creating an initial plan of action should something occur. In addition, she identified similar library settings to hers and requested copies of their emergency documents and received permission to use content from two websites that provided basic information. Asking her staff to assist her in selecting the best information or most relevant content from other libraries and web materials in the first six months of her management, Elspeth created a quick set of crucial policies and procedures. These addressed protection of her staff and constituents, brought in local emergency and first responder individuals in the community to provide a half-day workshop for staff, and asked the appropriate individuals to assess and recommend building signage regarding emergency management issues.

Elspeth had noted at her one-year anniversary with the organization that she needed to return to the emergency and disaster issues in earnest, identify dollars and bring together a team, and prepare a full-scale disaster plan and emergency management policies and procedures. Now, eighteen months into her tenure as manager, her work group was well underway to creating the appropriate "disaster and emergency management plan" for the library.

2. List the important or relevant facts or statements of the situation.

- The manager was a new manager and was aware of general needs, but, being new, was not as familiar with what the specific library needs.

- Files indicated materials were missing that are needed for disaster and emergency management and planning.
- The library was an older building.
- The library was on the seventh floor.
- The first approach to filling this void was the purchase of a medical emergency kit.
- Elspeth realized her lack of knowledge about the environment and identified staff to help her assess what was needed.
- Elspeth identified appropriate relevant documents and secured permission to use them.
- A "quick" set of emergency and disaster planning policies and procedures were identified, revised as needed, and produced for the interim until a more specific plan was created.
- Initial policies and procedures are produced for both staff and constituents.
- Elspeth identified outside expertise needed and arranged for quick, appropriate training for staff.
- Critical and required signage needed was identified, created, and posted.
- Temporary content was used "temporarily" (many people just create these with bigger plans in mind and then never get around to them) and almost immediately a work group got underway to create complete content.
- Elspeth identified cost issues and dollars to support this critical project.

3. List the characters or "players" in the situation, and list them in relevant categories. Several categories might be: those directly involved, those indirectly involved, and those affected by the situation.

Directly involved:

- Manager
- Staff—work group

- Staff—general/others
- Constituents, library users
- Other building tenants, especially those on the sixth and eighth floors
- Any building emergency personnel
- Workshop providers
- Signage expertise/individuals

Indirectly involved:

- Managers and workers on other floors in the building
- Umbrella organization individuals, such as Elspeth's manager and Elspeth's peers
- Benchmark/best practice content authors

Affected by the situation:

- Areas that may have less money because dollars are needed for this initiative

4. List the primary issues or problems in the situation.

- The library must have appropriate and required signage relating to emergency management and disaster planning. (See Appendix B)
- Individuals who work in the library must know what to do when emergencies or disasters happen.
- Individuals who use the library must know what to do when emergencies or disasters happen.
- Temporary policies, procedures, and plans are necessary but should be considered temporary and replaced in a timely fashion.

5. Given what you know, prioritize the issues or problems in the situation.

- Individuals who work in the library must know what to do when emergencies or disasters happen.

- Individuals who use the library must know what to do when emergencies or disasters happen.
- The library must have appropriate and required signage relating to emergency management and disaster planning. (See Appendix B)
- Temporary policies, procedures, and plans are necessary but should be considered temporary and replaced in a timely fashion.

6. After reviewing the situation, list "what can be done" or possible solutions for each issue or problem.

- Temporary documents can and should be used until other more "permanent" documents are completed.
- Elspeth should use staff members who are familiar with the environment to assist her in vetting outside plans.
- Outside expertise should be used for initial training on how temporary policies and procedures are to be used and how signage assists constituents in emergency and disaster situations.

7. List what can't be done, given any limitations or relevant facts. Match what can't be done with the relevant issues as needed.

- Managers can't "know nothing" and ignore missing and current policies and procedures, lack of content, and lack of policies and procedures.
- Managers can't rely on other building emergency personnel to create and/or maintain emergency and disaster content.
- Managers can't rely solely on other building emergency and/or disaster personnel to ensure attention and service is paid to staff designated to assist when needed.
- Managers can't rely solely on other building emergency and/or disaster personnel to ensure attention and service is paid to constituents present during emergency and disaster events.

8. Choose the best one or two solutions, matching up any solutions with what can't be done.

- Temporary documents can and should be used until other more "permanent" documents are completed.
- Elspeth should use staff members who are familiar with the environment to assist her in vetting outside plans to avoid using others' plans and not adjusting them for temporary or permanent use for the current library setting.
- Outside expertise should be used for initial training on how temporary policies and procedures are to be used and how signage assists constituents in emergency and disaster situations.

9. Speculate on the outcome if the solutions are put into effect.

- Temporary documents can and should be used until other more "permanent" documents are completed. *Managers, staff involved in the planning, and all staff in library should feel confident that they know what to do should an emergency situation or disaster occur.*
- Elspeth should use staff members who are familiar with the environment to assist her in vetting outside plans to avoid using others' plans and not adjusting them for temporary or permanent use for the current library setting. *Initial or temporary plans created are appropriate to the specific library setting and are useful in handling emergencies and disasters.*
- Outside expertise should be used for initial training on how temporary policies and procedures are to be used and how signage assists constituents in emergency and disaster situations. *Managers and staff are prepared to handle emergency or disaster issues and all constituents during and after the event.*

10. Build in an evaluation mechanism.

- Manager vets content
- Staff vets content

- Schedule and "grade" or assess practice events
- Staff self-evaluates their own performance at practice events
- Constituents evaluate practice events

11. Consider the need to have both short-range and long-range solutions.

- Short-range solutions should include using temporary documents until other more "permanent" documents are completed.
- Long-range solutions should include Elspeth using staff members who are familiar with the environment to assist her in vetting outside plans to avoid using others' plans and not adjusting them for temporary or permanent use for the current library setting. Outside expertise should be used for initial training on how temporary policies and procedures are to be used and how signage assists constituents in emergency and disaster situations.

12. Consider delegating all or part of an issue or problem (this might create changes in the process).

- Short-range solutions should include using temporary documents until other more "permanent" documents are completed. Therefore, Elspeth should delegate the organization of temporary documents to her administrative assistant who will work with her assistant director to organize and assess use for critiquing documents for more long-term use.
- Long-range solutions should include Elspeth using staff members who are familiar with the environment to assist her in vetting outside plans to avoid using others' plans and not adjusting them for temporary or permanent use for the current library setting. The vetting should be delegated to the Disaster Recovery Team. Outside expertise should be used for

initial training on how temporary policies and procedures are to be used and how signage assists constituents in emergency and disaster situations. The Disaster Recovery Team should consult Disaster Plan "vendors" in Appendix B, identify three local experts, and contracts with them to design training materials and to assist in vetting of short-term documents for long-term use.

12. Consider creating a time line for prioritized solutions (this might create changes). The Disaster Recovery Team sets up a two-track time line. The first time line includes:

- Vetting short term documents within the first three months.
- Beginning data gathering for long-term documents within the first three months.
- Identifying local experts and contacting them for future use.
- Assessing budget for future contracting with local experts.

The second time line includes:

- Designing Requests for Proposals (RFPs) for contracting with local experts.
- Assessing data gathered from short-term documents to design long-term documents.
- Designing long-term documents to be used in disaster planning and recovery.

LIBRARY ELEMENTS IN PLANNING, PREVENTION, RESPONSE, AND RECOVERY

Institutions need to determine their areas of responsibility in planning, prevention, response, and recovery of disasters and emergencies. In some institutions the environment or context in which the library exists controls all elements of emergency management and disaster recovery; others control only partial areas while yet others provide only umbrella organization documents and no control. In some situations, umbrella institutions or environments do not provide any content or documents while others do not have more standard umbrella institutions (such as 501c3 library environments), and in these cases, libraries must create all documents.

Although institutions have always taken emergency management and disaster recovery seriously, the events of the past decade have only heightened awareness of the need for attention to emergency management plans and disaster recovery documents. In turn, this has also increased documents design, the need for required policies, procedures, and documents, and training design for all sizes and types of libraries and information environments.

Library Managers

Library managers must assess environments to determine what emergency management and disaster recovery documents are needed, which documents are available from umbrella institutions or other individuals in the environment, what data needs to be gathered as part of emergency management and disaster recovery processes, what policies and procedures are needed, and what training is required. Additionally, of all the elements gathered, which items are determined by law and required, which are required in general, and which are recommended or optional.

Managers must ensure that content is integrated into other institutional processes, who or which positions have roles and responsibilities regarding these areas, and which data is needed and what processes are in place to ensure appropriate and correct data-gathering. Managers must also ensure that assessment and evaluation processes are in place, that local partnerships are identified and nurtured, and that budget dollars are requested and received.

Budgeting

Institutional budgets should be designed to include budget categories to support emergency management and disaster recovery activities, such as supplies, training (for example, conferences) training materials, equipment and hardware, software, and staffing dollars, including hourly (temporary) dollars and consulting (special expertise) dollars. In addition, general dollars are needed in purchasing and contracting for supporting dollars of system maintenance. Dollars should be appropriately distributed in operating vs. capital dollars and, as awarded, soft dollars from grants and outside dollars.

Risk Management

Risk management is part of the emergency management process and strives to manage risks through proactive (rather than crisis or reactive management) continuous assessment and decision-making to assist organizations in identifying the risks in an environment. Specifically, it identifies what could go wrong; creates strategies for dealing with risks; and determines and prioritizes which risks are important to deal with and in what order. Risk managers advise institutions in the design of policies and processes to not only reduce risk in general but also to invest in processes to reduce the costs of emergencies and disasters. Risk managers— either full-time, part-time or consultants in libraries—establish directions and create risk management teams to assist in continuous assessment, tracking, and control to effectively use program resources.

Risk management, in the world of nonprofit or library emergency management and disaster recovery, is not a new area of management but has increased in importance, size, and responsibility in the past decade. Although many institutions do not have the dollars needed or are of the size to have a full-time staff member in charge of risk management, risk issues should still be part of the emergency management and disaster recovery landscape. The goals of risk processes in libraries are the goals of risk managers in all types and sizes of institutions and include the prevention of problems, the integration of risk assessment, and management into library practices.

Library risk management elements include:

- Data destruction and consequences (catalog and constituent records)
- Equipment destruction (workstations and information appliances)
- Collection damage (print and media materials)

Risk management elements related to these library areas in the prevention mode include these examples:

- Assessment of the value of collections
- Design, implementation, and oversight of environmental needs, including warning systems and temperature control for safe collections
- Assessment of the replacement possibilities of damaged collections
- Cost of assessing cleaning and recovery
- Cost of cleaning and recovery
- Assistance in the design and maintenance of the Disaster Recovery Plan

Staff Roles and Responsibilities (Individuals, Organizational Design, Decision-making)

Library staff and additional individuals, such as volunteers, partners, and library supporters, play a number of roles in emergency management and disaster recovery. This includes sharing expertise for membership on disaster recovery teams, functional area, or departmental data gatherings for risk management information; budgeting for materials and resources; participating in training; assisting in recovery activities, such as cleaning collections (when appropriate); and serving as resource people for primary or secondary responsibilities (support for special needs employees or constituents).

Specifically, library examples of these roles and responsibilities that can be found in human resource documents include:

Individuals/Individual Positions within the Institution

- Team leader—disaster recovery (develops relationships, acts as process owner for documents)
- Team member—disaster recovery
- Expert/resource person—collection assessment, collection recovery
- Facilities/evacuation manager—by floor, by department
- Facilities/evacuation manager—special populations (constituents, employees)
- Facilities/evacuation manager backup—special populations (constituents, employees)
- Communication/media manager—general and specific to emergency management and disaster recovery (process owner for communication system, including contact information)
- Safety and security manager—may handle materials and resources
- Business manager—process owner for financial resources and insurance issues
- Systems manager—hardware, software, data

Emergency Management and/or Disaster Recovery Team/Committee

Although one team might write a plan while another team might carry it out, those activities best carried out in teams include:

- Analyzing, benchmarking, and designing the institution's strategic plan for emergency management and disaster recovery
- Designing assessment and performance measurements for disaster mitigation, preparedness, response, and recovery policies and procedures
- Designing business continuity plans
- Assessing risks within the environment on an ongoing basis
- Establishing ongoing workgroups for assistance in disaster mitigation, preparedness, response, and recovery
- Overseeing training and exercises, communication plans, hard and soft dollars for budgeting and finance

Membership on the team might include representatives from umbrella institutions or community members, such as law enforcement, facilities, network services, human resources, health, media/communications, risk management staff, legal, and all staff levels.

Facilities

In the complicated processes and study of emergency management and disaster recovery, library facilities are:

- Environments that are damaged and destroyed.
- Environments that can be used for meeting places for businesses or families in times of emergency.
- Temporary gathering places during evacuation.
- Environments that can be shelter-in-place locations for employees, library constituents, and individuals from the community or the umbrella areas of the institutions.

Library facilities should be designed and built for prevention or mitigation and minimization of disasters. In the absence of the opportunity to build a building that meets prevention recommendations, they should be assessed and renovated to better face emergencies and disasters. Although costs vary dramatically, prevention designs or renovations can include these examples:

- Shelving installation
- Placement of materials on shelves
- Entrance/door seals
- Window seals
- Window materials
- Landscaping
- Parking lot conditions and surfaces
- Power installation/protection

Additional library facility issues also include access and closure policies. Libraries work on guidelines for access and closing with umbrella institutions or governing bodies (through first responders and community safety leaders); however, standards and norms related to closing environment policies for activities and events (before, during, and after) have changed dramatically over the past two decades. Managers might imagine that with increased methods and speedy communications, it might be easier to make the closure decisions; the reality is that many other issues are involved. And, as with any other emergency management decision, there are a variety of categories to consider.

These categories for libraries to consider include:

- What are access issues?
- What are the different levels of access?
- Who makes access decisions?
- What are access time lines for decisions?
- What are access recommendations?

What are the different levels of access to consider? These include "no access/complete closure to staff and general public"; "no access to the public; limited access to staff"; "limited access to the public; limited access to staff"; and "full access to public and staff."

Policies and Procedures

The practices of emergency management and disaster recovery include dozens of issues that dictate either sections in existing policies and procedures or those that are specific and unique to the issues. In libraries, policies and procedures specific to these areas include:

- Human resources documents, including job descriptions and evaluations
- Statements on training (required and recommended)
- Risk management content
- Facilities usage

Library policies and procedures should have content integrated into them to include:

- Customer service
- Communication
- Community partnerships
- Collection management

Forms, Checklists, and Charts

The world of disaster recovery and emergency management has literally hundreds of different kinds of forms, checklists, and charts recommended for institutions. These documents are recommended for events and activities (before, during, and after), and the information must be maintained in print and online in multiple locations and with multiple copies. Emergency management resources include many examples of these forms to be used in prevention, preparation, and handling or management during the event as well as a myriad of postevent activities. Although forms in each area of emergency management have unique aspects, general statements about forms can be made. These general statements can be used to assess existing management documents as well as to design documents.

General statements:

1. The obvious primary recommendation is "make sure you have all the forms you need." This can be achieved in a number of ways; however, the easiest is "another form," a checklist of forms needed for emergency management. These checklists are found in a number of places (see Appendix A for websites and other sources), and this "master form" can be arranged by the "stages of" or "typical activities" within emergency management. Examples include a checklist for "prevention" that would list supplies (needed, stored, used) and prevention assessment (building security, safety, etc.).

2. All forms must be placed on a strict review and revision schedule that must be adhered to within organizations. This schedule needs to include review of the primary organization's forms as well as review of time lines from related partners and ancillary organizations.

3. Form content must remain current and reflect new issues about emergency events; different needs for those managing the events; new/changing resources, such as equipment and software; facilities issues; staffing issues; general organizational changes, such as shifting functions; new titles; new job descriptions; and collaborative issues and changes, such as new media contacts, expanded or different community partners, or differences or changes in the emergency elements themselves. An example of the latter might be new or different identified fire hazards (as a result of building construction

or changes in equipment), and thus new fire extinguishers purchased that dictate different training.

4. Forms must be designed to be read and comprehended at the lowest reading levels possible given form content. Although a general rule of thumb is words three syllables or less, forms must avoid colloquialisms, oblique "insider" information or references, initialisms, acronyms, and references to "who does what" by name of individual rather than by title for the greatest, easiest level of comprehension. Individuals reading and using forms should not have to "guess" what something means. (See "signs" for related information.)

5. Forms must be available in complete sets in a variety of formats, such as online and print as well as backup content in formats, including CDs. As much as possible the format, size, and general "look" of forms should be replicated across platforms. Individuals managing an event should be able to use print forms, and they should be identical to online forms; that is, avoid having a one-page print form from online sources print out as a two-page form. Preferred online content might be in PDF form to expand possibilities for exact duplication. Literally, no matter where the forms come from, everyone needs to be on the same page.

6. There is a great likelihood that duplication of forms (printing and photocopying) will not be possible before, during, or after events due to loss of power. Forms should be assessed for critical needs for "now rather than later" duplication of content on completed forms, and those forms deemed necessary should be created as "carbon" copy forms.

7. Credentialing forms (like credentialing signs) is critical for users and includes forms having space for indicating (initials, codes, and titles) who completes the form, and in some cases, indicating all who handled or used the form during the event. "All who handled" might include management identification, monitors, or assessor identification.

8. Forms must have space for legends to explain abbreviations, signatures or "sign-offs," titles, and so forth, and, in general, meanings needed for in-house or unique information from the primary organization or partners.
9. Forms must be assessed to determine if multiple languages are needed on some or all forms.
10. Forms must be assessed to determine if graphics are needed to illustrate issues on some or all forms.
11. Print forms should be designed for standard sizes of notebooks (or equivalent) for ease of use, duplication, and distribution.
12. Online forms should be designed for web environments; however, the design should also ensure that content can be printed and used without need for revision or reformatting and can be used in standard sizes of notebooks for ease of use, duplication, and distribution.
13. Form designs should avoid using elements that do not reproduce easily (colors or ink in general, multiple colors, and color of paper).
14. Form designs should avoid using elements that illustrate ideas but do not reproduce easily or at all (complicated charts or ideas defined by colors that don't duplicate).

Form samples in Appendix B include:

- Management issues/audit
- Special needs/special populations audit
- Who to call/inform
- Contact list/phone tree—security
- Experts
- Sign in sheets/keeping/taking role
- If /then forms
- Vendors

EMERGENCY/DISASTER ACTION PLANS

CONTENTS

- Scenario: Disaster Plan—Design and Implementation
- Scenario: Disaster Plan—Using Disaster Plans and Planning Resources
- Designing Disaster Plans/Action Documents
- Disaster Plan Introduction
- Definitions of Terms
- Weather Systems, Weather, and Destructive Elements Caused by Weather Systems
- Man-made Events
- Emergency Communication Policies, Procedures and Processes, and Systems Recovery
- Choosing Disaster Planning Resources
- Best Practices: Disaster Plans

EMERGENCY/DISASTER ACTION PLANS

SCENARIO: DISASTER PLAN—DESIGN AND IMPLEMENTATION

Flooding in the Midwest, school shootings in the South, and bomb threats on the West Coast prompted the Ridgemont School District to form a committee to prepare the district for disasters and emergencies whether they were caused by a "human factor," weather, or geological elements. The decision to address the need for planning, however, was stymied by the governing board members who were divided in a 50–50 split on *how* to prepare the district. Although all agreed that attention needed to be paid, no one felt comfortable with how to begin the process.

The committee had its first meeting in two weeks, and Principal Richards was tapped by the superintendent to lead the committee in planning for the unexpected.

Questions:

- What should Richards do first to prepare himself for the committee?
- What should Richards do to prepare committee members?
- What should be done to organize the committee during the meeting?
- What should happen after the meeting?

Questions/Answers:

What should Richards do first to prepare himself for the committee?

1. Interview the superintendent to determine her specific needs for the committee.
2. Gather additional information by interviewing others recommended by the superintendent, including the goals of the governing board.
3. Contact community organizations that deal with "human factor" and natural disasters for historical data and statistics on the likelihood of area disasters.
4. Draft a charge for the committee and run it past the superintendent for final content.
5. Identify print and online content for committee members, including specific geographic information and best practices from the area that are generally recognized as quality district documents.
6. Include recommended documents from other committees.

What should Richards do to prepare committee members?

1. Contact committee members, welcome them to the group, create an electronic list for communication as well as a wiki for sharing, and assess group strengths and weaknesses for communication and technology for designing training materials.
2. Distribute a charge incorporating superintendent and board vision and goals to the committee and post it to the e-list and wiki.
3. Assess and organize content to provide members with background information and resources available through community organizations and recommended documents from other committees.

4. Create an agenda, package the charge and the documents, and distribute to the committee.
5. Design a blank time line for the committee; request that committee members bring their calendars for setting future dates.
6. Prepare name tags.
7. Create a note-taking form from the agenda.

What should be done to organize the committee during the meeting?

1. Manage a "meet and greet."
2. Introduce committee members.
3. Choose a notetaker.
4. Distribute/identify package contents for committee.
5. Review/discuss and revise charge as necessary.
6. Brainstorm goals.
7. Discuss time line.
8. Discuss training needed.
9. Establish future meetings.
10. Assign homework for reading content, locating other content, and reviewing websites.
11. Collect minutes/notes.

What should happen after the meeting?

1. Review notes, prepare items for distribution, including draft calendar, project time line, and homework assignments.
2. Send revised charge to superintendent and board for approval.
3. Organize training needed.
4. Post thank-you notes to e-mail lists.
5. Drop content into wiki.
6. Sign up for future locations for meetings.

7. Match time line to district needs.
8. Check back with members to see if they have questions or have needs to be met.
9. Send out tentative agenda and workplace for the next meeting.
10. Follow up on training delivered, completed, and ensuing questions.
11. Query area institutions for their use of disaster plans.
12. Meet with the umbrella institution staff in emergency management and disaster recovery (if they aren't on the committee, request they attend as a guest and be present for historical information and area lessons learned).

SCENARIO: DISASTER PLAN—USING DISASTER PLANS AND PLANNING RESOURCES

When Carmen got the 2:00 a.m. call from the Lakewood Fire Department that the "library was on fire," she immediately went to her home office laptop, pulled the flash drive of library planning documents out of the drawer, and accessed the library's disaster plan that was completed last summer.

Although the fire captain had told her that he could not give her a status report until the fire was contained, Carmen began to hurriedly scan the document to reacquaint herself with her recommended "first steps."

Questions:

• What are Carmen's first steps from 2:00 a.m. until the time when the library should be opened the next morning?
• What does Carmen's first day of work after the fire look like?
• What sections of the disaster plan does Carmen use first?

DESIGNING DISASTER PLANS/ACTION DOCUMENTS

The cornerstone of mitigating, preparing for, preventing, managing, and recovering from disasters is the content gathered, identified, vetted, mounted/published and distributed, continuously updated, used, and then evaluated. Typically this content is organized into a plan that serves as a repository, buying guide, action plan, and evaluative tool usually identified as a "disaster plan." Along with plan content, the flexibility of how content is arranged, maintained, and accessed is always of paramount concern along with the need for plans to be translated into appropriate languages and available in diverse formats for differently-abled employees and constituents.

Content Gathered

Gathering content on disaster prevention, management, and recovery has significantly improved with the ease of publishing and distribution. While more traditional ways of selecting sources are still sound, literally dozens of newer ways of gathering data are now used. These ways include:

- Using a monograph to provide direction and content on disaster planning in general
- Gathering periodicals on one aspect or various aspects of the disaster planning process
- Using bibliographies and webliographies from monographs, periodicals, and websites
- Using recommended, best practices, or benchmark data (in general or specifically related to other entities on this list)
- Using professional association-recommended content
- Requesting disaster planning examples recommended by consultants, experts, and peers

- Requesting disaster planning examples from similar institutions
- Purchasing template (.com) disaster plans
- Hiring consultants and experts
- Attending professional development, continuing education, and training programs and events focusing on disaster planning (including individual programs, workshops, and classes)
- Interviewing individuals who have experienced various aspects of disasters

Content Identified

After content is gathered, organizations usually find they have too much information to use and must narrow down the content to meet their needs. While the perfect answer or "best practice" might appear to be to select only similar organizations' plans, the reality is that type of library, size of collection, or governance structure might be the last factors on your list when choosing the best example of a disaster plan.

Typically the best choice is to create a profile that matches the likelihood of disaster types given geological and geographic locations, age of facilities, numbers of employees, formats of resources, and budgets for preparedness and prevention as well as budgets available for recovery. These elements, not coincidentally, are often the major determining factors for insurance choices, premiums, and risk assessments.

Content Vetted

Often librarians are too "close" to their environment and lack disaster planning skills to assess content to create a specific disaster plan. Assessing or vetting content for application to specific environments, therefore, is better done by other employees within the umbrella organization—peers, consultants, and/or members of advisory boards or experts identified from groups. Matching content can also be achieved by finding a workshop where outcomes include building organizational profiles and outlines of disaster plans.

All plans include content that offer different disaster scenarios, such as smoke damage versus fire and smoke damage or leaking versus a major flood. Other recommended approaches to creating plans include creating more than one scenario or profile of a plan that might represent, for example, two plans with two different sums of available money; two plans with existing staff and available individuals, another plan with significant community members trained for disaster planning assistance; and one plan with little assistance from umbrella organizations.

Content Mounted/Published and Distributed

Historically plans have been bound but have perforated pages or loose pages in notebook sleeves that can be easily removed for forms, templates, checklists, buying guides, and so on. Contemporary processes include plans that:

- Are printed using formulas for numbering pages (similar to loose-leaf legal documents) and widely distributed
- Are printed and placed in binders or notebooks and widely distributed
- Are placed on websites on institutional internal and external web environments (with print copies widely distributed) and easily updated
- Are placed on websites on institutional internal and external web environments and are able to be searched and easily updated
- Are burned to CDs for maximizing durability of format, protection of content during disasters and ease of use
- Are placed on free web wikis for ease of use, protection of

content during disasters, staff training, and expert input and updating with print copies widely distributed
- Are placed on subscription wikis to maintain confidentiality, protection of content during disasters, staff training, and expert input and updating with print copies widely distributed

Obviously, with the growth of online and web-related avenues for mounting documents and publication, great concern must be taken for duplicating online content in print, the process of print distribution, and the systematic updating of print documents. Recommended approaches to mounting and publishing documents include the creation of a secure web environment that allows for maximum input and that is designed to allow easy duplication and updating. Additionally, subscribing to higher-end wikis that allow for customized design and updating as well as maximum document additions and use of media are preferred. (Newer media formats such as blogs are usable if the blogs are higher-end subscription resources with maximum customization that allows for content to be organized in methods beyond traditional blog postings.)

Content Continuously Updated

Disaster plans contain both classic, standardized, and little or seldom changing content as well as content that needs continuous updating. Given the importance of this plan and the range of content, organizations need to consider the most important part of the process, which is the selection of the process owner. Once the plan is designed, this person has primary responsibility for creating a process to continuously update content and inform members of the organization and beyond when the most important content has changed. Changing elements that would NOT need to be disseminated in a systematic fashion would include areas such as vendor updates and formulas used in recovery cleaning. Those areas that would include dissemination would be changes in personnel involved in the process, the contact information part of the communication plan, and individuals in the umbrella organization identified as assisting in the process.

Techniques for continuous updating include:

- Assessing and tagging plan areas that need to be watched closely
- Establishing a timetable for proactively reviewing content identified as critical or time-sensitive
- Identifying processes in place that automatically update content such as websites with RSS feeds
- Identifying software elements of resources, such as automatic updating e-lists when contents are altered or added
- Using software indexing, such as the identification of cloud tags (subject tags) for websites and keyword descriptors (wikis)
- Identifying organizations that have established standardized updates, such as professional associations
- Identifying individuals with specific content area expertise to assist in updating

Finally, although significant systems and processes may be in place for updating the plan, identifying HOW readers know the plan is updated is critical. An updating "legend" should be provided that indicates the following section by section:

- When the plan was visited and reviewed
- When sections were used and for what purpose
- When sections were reviewed and revised
- When sections were reviewed and had major changes, substitutions, or additions of content or sections

Content Used

Because today's disaster plans have expanded information, especially in the area of preparedness and prevention, managers and plan process owners need to establish ways of tracking what areas of the plan are used and how they are used. Examples of prevention and preparedness uses as well as examples that go beyond "disasters" include the following.

- In designing new facilities or choosing new or replacing existing HVAC systems, plans offer parameters of heating and cooling, such as highs and lows for air quality and prevention of mold growth.
- Stack maintenance includes maintaining dust-free shelves and resources, and plans offer recommendations for cleaning solutions for "home grown" as well as acceptable commercial products.
- Choosing sustainability as a library goal dictates consulting plan-recommended "green" resources products and processes, such as recycling.
- Plan sections should have methods of noting when content is used, how often it is used, and if it is used for what it is intended.

Content Evaluated

Part of content use, tracking when content is used, how often it is used, and if it is used for what it is intended is an assessment and evaluation component to determine if what is in the plan is accurate and successful. Evaluation standards should be determined and could include a Likert scale assessment of sections and items as well as a more qualitative assessment that includes, for example, perception and opinion. Examples include:

Likert Scale Assessment

- On a scale of 1 to 5 (low to high respectively), rate the usefulness of the cleaning solvent used in cleaning metal shelving.
- Select the appropriate response for assessing the contact/telephone tree used to notify staff of library closures.
  - All addresses and numbers in the contact/telephone tree worked perfectly.
  - Several of the addresses and numbers were not accurate, and staff could not be reached.
  - Over one half the addresses and numbers were not accurate, and staff could not be reached.

Perception and Opinion

- Did staff exhibit appropriate behavior in speaking with the press about the library closure due to the (fill in the disaster event)? If no, list examples where communication was inappropriate.
- Once the disaster event passed, were first responders sensitive to resource issues during recovery? If no, list examples of lack of sensitivity to resources during recovery.

DISASTER PLAN INTRODUCTION

The plan "Introduction" should indicate the purpose and focus of the plan and can be specific and include a charge to the individual or team tasked to complete the plan. It could indicate the format of the plan (basic template, guide, handbook, manual, or reference tool) and when the document should be used (prior to events, during operational planning, when designing strategic plans, when building budgets, or in the event of a disaster or emergency and / or dealing with threats). It could also list the audience as well as "players" (internal and external employees, partners, peers, community members, constituents), resources and services (facilities, all materials and resources, data), support infrastructure (role of umbrella institution, primary responders, experts, media, vendors, and suppliers), and types of disasters and emergencies in question as well as specific approaches to address events, activities, disasters, and emergencies.

In addition, the "Introduction" can include or can precede general categories of preparation and response to situations with summary information.

Mitigation and Prevention

Mitigation and prevention terms are often used synonymously and, although these terms are not really synonyms, any one of these terms can be used for the "pre" category of "pre" disaster or emergency. In general, this category of emergency management and disaster recovery is designed to guide employees to think ahead of situations, to both plan and take action to reduce risks and minimize opportunities for activities to take place at all (spills, toxic reactions, fires, flooding), and to define actions that prepare environments so that if emergencies and disasters occur, damage is reduced. Aspects of "pre" include writing, planning, relationships, organization, and training. It also specifically includes relationships (experts, first responders, media, peer institutions, umbrella organization departments/managers, and vendors) and assessments and services (hazard identification, environmental and facilities audits for safety, violence prevention opportunities and strategies, historical incident review and assessment, and assessment for vulnerability, etc.).

Preparedness

Although preparedness is often (and can be) grouped with mitigation and prevention, preparedness typically indicates more specific planning and organization once data from mitigation and prevention has been gathered. It includes assessing and vetting of data gathered in mitigation and prevention, reviewing other plans, and crafting the institution's approach to events and activities. In addition to gathering data, partners, constituents, and other stakeholders are identified, roles and responsibilities are clarified, and training is designed and delivered.

During the preparedness phase, all media and communications are designed for all internal, external, and potential constituents; policies and procedures are identified and customized as needed, including media and communication generated by the institution as well as communication generated by outside entities. These necessitate specialized devices, such as weather radios and/or ham radios and processes for identifying, recording, and tracking constituents who are chosen by using sign-in sheets, constituent databases, name tags/identifiers, and so on. Communication trees or processes are established to include older telephone trees, cell phones for texting, IM, e-mail and twittering. Facility floor plans and safe spaces/lockdown/shelter for constituents, storage, and existing and alternative energy needs are also identified. Emergency/disaster equipment and supplies are identified, budgeted for, purchased, organized, stored, and training is identified and carried out as needed.

Response

Responding to crises and disasters varies dramatically; therefore, plans vary dramatically. During these events, employee safety, constituent safety, and business continuity are paramount, and all specifics of disasters and emergencies are identified, assessment and recordkeeping forms are put into play, systems and processes (for example, communication) are activated; needed constituent responses are chosen and implemented, medical needs are identified and administered, supplies are accessed, and use is tracked.

Recovery

Obviously the recovery period is defined in direct relationship to the nature, type, and severity of the disaster or emergency as well as the success of previously created plans. Along with major and more systematic recovery strategies—assessing activities, establishing recovery time lines, insurance and risk management operations, debriefing all individuals with roles and responsibilities as well as those affected by the event or by event aspects, repairing facilities and restocking supplies restoring business operations (establishing continuity), and reestablishing infrastructure—comes major concerns for the reestablishment of employee and constituent activity as well as the importance of reestablishing a balanced and emotionally sound work environment.

Additional related issues include budgeting for restocking, assessing data gathered and data-gathering tools as well as anecdotal data for "lessons learned" for additional planning and future training. Finally, institutions should plan for both facilities and constituent "anniversaries," for assessing repairs "holding" for safe business, as well as the emotional issues of dealing with memories and anniversary dates.

Priorities

Disaster plan "Introductions" should also include priorities for organizations. These priorities are determined by the institution's identification and decision regarding "what is prepared for" and "what is saved or recovered first"? The priorities provide direction for organizing the plans themselves as well as direction for training, budgeting, and planning. Examples of "priorities" include:

- Safety of employees and constituents is paramount.
- Alerting mechanisms are the first purchasing and maintenance funding priority (weather radios, ham radios, emergency message board systems).

- Media collections are the first collection to be removed and recovered.
- Resource data (databases and digital collections) are assessed prior to organizational data (for example, patron identification and circulation records).
- Hardware is evacuated prior to furniture.

DEFINITIONS OF TERMS

Definitions of terms or glossaries are typically found at the end of the content. However, in disaster plans, knowledge of and easy identification and referral to terms are of critical importance in training and media/communications. Although many definitions are classic or seldom-changing information, the terms section or "glossary" should be reviewed as frequently if not more frequently for revisions and additions.

Categories of Emergencies and Disasters

Emergencies and disasters must be categorized in order to train and to be able to identify levels of impact and plans for recovery. In addition, specific categorization allows for standardized assessment and documentation. (For "documentation" information see appendix B.) No further designations (for example, natural vs. man-made) have been included because so many events/activities are intermingled and related to each other.

Earthquakes

Although some warnings are possible for earthquakes and some geographic locations are prone to earthquakes, many areas also suffer significant effects from earth movements. Although preventing earthquakes is impossible, there is extensive work that can be done——from construction to training—to mitigate damage.

Many websites (see appendix A) exist with extensive content on preparation and safety during and recovery from earth movements and minor and major earthquakes. Additional damages or collateral damage from earthquakes include fire; major events categorized as flood events, such as tsunamis; other water damages and effects from combinations of events; and structural damage including mold and pestilence.

Fires

Fires can be either a man-made or a natural disaster. Prevention is possible by utilizing fire prevention, mitigation, control or management, and recovery techniques. Extensive web-based fire prevention information (as show in appendix A) offers lists of critical needs, including the importance of drills for evacuation and recovery, smoke detectors, fire alarm systems, fire extinguishers, sprinkler systems, roles and responsibilities, and training. Fire prevention and recovery must include fire, ash, and smoke damage as well as damage from water or chemical treatment. Fires can also be caused by storms and lightning, and this damage might necessitate recovery involving water from the storm as well.

Floods

Floods can be either a man-made or natural disaster. Not only can they happen on any floor of a building but can also occur on the floor or from the ceiling and can take place in any part of the country at any time of year. Although there are many preventive actions, water is "tricky" and can emanate from plumbing, HVAC (heating, ventilating, and air conditioning) systems, roof, window, gutter and general facility leaks, and accidental causes, such as open windows. It can also arise from environmental floods and flash floods due to weather and weather systems, bodies of water, and water leaving bodies of water to enter into grounds or facilities. Major issues with leaks and flooding come from the source of the water and the particular clean-up elements that must be used to clean up both the immediate and residual problems associated with water. In addition, related issues are running water versus standing water, the water's contact with a material, and the length of time the water is IN areas while either running or standing, and the temperature of the environment while the water flows or stands in a location. Although prior notification may be possible, typically there is little warning. Flood insurance is often expensive and general insurance policies should be scrutinized to identify coverage for flood and water damage from any of the possibilities in the "flood" category.

Insects and Rodents

Infestations of insects and rodents in institutions may be due to facility issues, book/print materials issues, weather, or other issues such as food. Prevention is critical for addressing insects and rodent issues, including repairing facilities, setting traps, standardizing cleaning, spraying for insects (general and specific), and striving for food-free environments. Public postings of preventive processes must accompany mitigation and prevention treatment as well as recovery.

Along with recovery information, institutions are recommended to access professional literature on preservation and conservation that includes treatment and recovery content.

Landslides

Landslides can be caused by geological formations, from other natural disasters (fire, flood, earthquakes, volcanoes), and also can be "man-made" from construction or treatment of natural resources, such as clearing land or logging. Typically during a rapidly developing disaster, some prevention is possible if enough lead time is available. With a difficult recovery from excessive forces of nature, cleanup is challenging. As with flooding, the mix of elements within the landslide and the length of time material remains within the institution affects materials and resources.

Mold

Although mold is not unusual, mold can be caused by a wide variety of unusual elements. Typically, a lethal combination of events and activities that can cause mold are water, humidity, a lack of sun, inappropriate lighting, and heating and cooling issues. Unfortunately, there are tens of thousands of types of mold, and mold can form on almost any substance. Fortunately, this disaster has a number of preventive steps so that emergencies and disasters, given normal operations, can be minimized. The reality is, however, mold can grow when abnormal events and activities occur in a wide range of minor to major circumstances such as prolonged rain, a poorly regulated HVAC system, a small leak, materials with mold intermingled with materials that do not have mold, a materials' spill, and, obviously, a major flood.

There are many formulas and cleaning products designed specifically to deal with these situations, and many organizations in mold-prone areas are using contract help for specific cleaning needs to maintain maximum safety conditions for employees and constituents. Just as there are standardized schedules and public notices for treatment, like insect spraying, public notice should be posted for other treatments, such as mold mitigation, prevention, or abatement. This notification is for both employees and constituents and should take place whether the mold or treatment is in public or private areas, including storage environments.

Along with recovery information, institutions are recommended to access professional literature on preservation and conservation that includes treatment and recovery content.

Tornado and Tornadic Activity

Tornadoes are rotating clouds in or near storms with high winds and funnel activity. They can be very dangerous and destructive and vary in size and severity. Warnings are issued statements called either "watch" or "warning." As with other emergencies, institutions need extensive planning for constituent safety within a building for a short term, a safe place during an event or activity, and long-term evacuation location for employees and constituents. Although most emergency management regarding tornadoes covers events and post events, there is a list of prevention activities (see appendix A) for facilities design, including placement of doors and windows as well as expanse of glass, types of window/glass purchases, special installations, and roofing material choices.

Volcanoes

Although volcanoes occur in only a few areas, this event can cause or trigger other disasters like earth movements, earthquakes, floods, and landslides. Institutions located in areas where volcanoes or the effects of volcanoes are possible may find that a number of related elements might occur, including fire and the destruction of air quality (ash and smoke) as well as related problems due to the treatment—meaning water damage or chemical treatment—applied for halting fires.

WEATHER SYSTEMS, WEATHER, AND DESTRUCTIVE ELEMENTS CAUSED BY WEATHER SYSTEMS

Conditions

This section includes hurricanes, tornadoes, and other "nonstandard" weather elements, such as tsunamis as well as more standard storms or thunderstorms or winter and/or summer weather conditions. In general, designing plans for weather activities focuses on communication plans with alerting systems (weather radios, ham radios, shelter-in-place issues, evacuation issues, and prevention actions taken for facilities, including window choice and treatments, care of trees surrounding buildings, and of course, insurance).

Although most people think of major storms as being the only or at least the primary weather concern, professional emergency management and disaster planning literature includes many types of weather conditions that necessitate small and large equipment, alternate HVAC issues, facility add-ons (sealing as well as unique purchases and installations for doors and windows), and seasonal treatments (covering pipes and storm windows). These weather activities can be subdivided by seasons; however, different parts of the country experience seasonal activities at dramatically different times. These weather activities include wind chill, moderate snow (if areas are not used to snow), snow pellets like graupel, blizzards, blue northers, excessive rain, freezing rain, sleet, and downbursts (also called microbursts or macrobursts, depending on the range of storm activity). Additional weather activities include dry line (increases the likelihood of thunderstorms,) gust front or cold front, hailstones, lightning, severe thunderstorms (designated as severe based on wind speed and possible presence of rain/water, lightning, and hail), squall lines, straight line winds (can be as destructive as thunderstorms and tornadoes), supercells (thunderstorms with tornadic activity), and black ice (affects transportation but can also affect constituents walking into/out of buildings).

Standard Weather Language

In order to effectively manage events and activities, disaster and emergency management language needs to be understood and used by everyone involved. Typical language includes "watch," used by the National Weather Service for extreme weather, including tornadoes and tornadic activity, thunderstorms, or flooding. Watch is the broader term and is the initial warning. "Warning," used by the National Weather Service for the same or similar activities, is a secondary alert, and, as the more serious alert, refers to a situation where at least one of the emergency conditions already exists and has been spotted on radar. "Advisory" alerts are issued by the National Weather Service and are used when weather conditions are likely to cause negative situations or inconveniences and become hazardous. "Winter storm warnings" are issued by the National Weather Service to communicate hazardous and/or possibly life-threatening weather, including storms and ice. Finally, "winter storm watches" are issued by the National Weather Service and alert individuals to the risk of hazardous and life-threatening weather.

MAN-MADE EVENTS

Other emergency management and disaster recovery issues that in some arenas are classified as "man-made" include issues, events, and activities that have been "around" for many years but (post-9/11) are increasing in frequency and intensity. They include broadly defined health issues, such as pandemics, employee and constituent "suspicious behavior," terrorism, terrorism-related activities, and man-made and natural hazardous materials.

Pandemics

The presence and nature of pandemics varies throughout the world. Although the United States is typically not at risk for some of the global pandemics, there are elements that should be addressed, including influenza viruses and other viruses, such as Severe Acute Respiratory Syndrome (SARS). Public environments are always at risk for spreading infection, and institutions should focus on prevention. Prevention activities are outlined in disaster plans and should include health professional education and training for employees on infection issues when working with the public, cleaning time lines and processes, cleaning supply lists, policies and procedures (such as NOT letting the public use library phones at all or not without cleaning procedures in place), routine activities for cleaning public and employee equipment, and sick and illness policies and procedures for staff as well as signage for public environments. In addition, controlling illness and infection should include the purchase of, for example, some type of infection control kit, specific cleaning materials, first aid and safety kits, and in extreme circumstances, facemasks, and gloves (latex and nonlatex) for use in cleaning.

Managers in general, risk personnel, or designated emergency management employees should become acquainted with global, federal, state, and local health organizations as well as any umbrella institution health departments to monitor health information for standard and specialized prevention and to alert management and staff as needed.

Suspicious Behavior

Although it might be argued that "suspicious behavior" is hard to identify, categorize, and report, in reality there are a number of activities and events that *do* systematically characterize suspicious behavior. A review of these activities and events should serve to belie the criticism that the identification of suspicious behavior is solely from negative profiling of individuals based on color, perceived economic level, race, gender, and so on.

Generally in institutions "someone found where they are not supposed to be" is the first element of identifying suspicious behavior, and employees should identify and make very clear distinctions by signage and instruction, those parts of institutions that are not for use or entrance by the public without permission or credentials. Disaster plans and all employee education and training as well as signage should indicate access or lack of access through either universal language picture identification or multiple languages areas. Obvious areas include private offices, employee break spaces, storage areas, technology-staging areas, stairwells (labeled only for emergencies), and administrative offices (without permission); not-so-obvious areas include behind circulation desks and reference desks.

Additional issues related to suspicious behavior include suspicious things, suspicious people, frequency over time, distance, and an individual's—for lack of a better word—gut feelings or instinct based on experience or longevity in the work environment.

Questions for employees to ask themselves regarding being alert to suspicious events/activities and/or people:

- What is that item? Vehicle? Backpack? Luggage? Package? Supposed to be there? This relates to "there" in a specific location unattended *or* "there" as it relates to near something unusual such as "under a stairwell" or "next to an air vent."
- Is "that" supposed to be there at that time of day?
- Why might that person be behaving in such an unexpected manner? Individuals should not *just* be on the alert for odd clothing, for example, but also normal clothing, odd behavior, uniforms, and clipboards at an odd time of day. That manner might also be taking pictures or videos or using recording equipment. This is a harder "call" these days because of the inexpensive nature as well as the size of equipment *and* the combination of equipment with handheld devices.
- Why is that person there every day? Or again? Or in the same place for a fourth day in a row?
- Why is that same person in different but unusual places? For three days in a row? Or why is that person someone I don't know but in all the places I am in, at work?
- Be alert to comments or questions, such as "That strikes me as odd" or "That's not the way it's supposed to be . . . is it?" Employees should be trained and educated in the value of in-

stinct and gut feelings. Paying attention to personal instincts, signals, or triggers is not a bad thing and often pays off in identifying potentially negative or dangerous situations.

Finally, institutions should provide policies and processes and training in them for employees to report any of the behaviors described above in a timely fashion and under the auspices of the law. These policies and processes should outline the appropriate processes for security and law enforcement involvement, confidentiality of reporting and documentation or the lack thereof, and the specifics of handling any items related to terrorism activities.

Terrorism and Terrorism-related Activities

Given recent legislation and federal guidelines, a greater number of areas fit under the "terrorism" umbrella and as such are covered in disaster plans and emergency management. In fact, several areas in the general list, such as "fire," "pandemics," and "suspicious behavior" as well as "nuclear, biological, and chemical weapons" could also be placed in the terrorism category of the disaster plan. In general, however, this category includes explosions, bombs and bomb threats (in writing, over the phone, or in person), and hazardous materials leaks/fumes (for example, airborne, through the mail, and in packages) as well as biological and chemical weapons.

Post-9/11, "how to handle" situations specific to terrorism or related to terrorism are governed by legislation. Institutions are governed by these guidelines, and procedures are followed at local levels that are governed by (typically county) offices staffed by the FBI and, when appropriate, the CIA. General information on how to handle these situations can be found in federal agency content, specifically "homeland defense" and "emergency management." When working with employees to educate and train on terrorism, content from "suspicious behavior," "fire," and "hazardous materials" portions of the disaster plan should be used. In this section of the plan, specific policies and procedures from federal legislation are included.

Hazardous Materials—Man-made and Natural

Technically, hazardous materials are found everywhere, including cleaning materials, hardware cartridges, and batteries to name but a few. In fact, some materials are not hazardous until combined or affected by temperature changes. In addition, some materials become hazardous over time. In general materials should be purchased carefully, combined with great caution, labeled carefully, and stored carefully. Materials can become hazardous prior to purchase, during use, during storage, and while transporting between or among locations; typically, these materials must be disposed of according to local laws.

While prevention is an important part of the hazardous materials process, education and training are critical to provide employees with must and should statements and most importantly "don'ts." This training should also include protective clothing, unique handling, combination issues, and consequences that include damage to the environment/area, temporary but serious illness, long-lasting health effects, serious injury, and death. Hazardous materials can be found in explosives, poisons, combustible substances, and radioactive materials.

Online content in federal agency websites as well as health-related content is available, and one of the most important aspects of this content is continuous updating that includes tracking of historical, existing, and new materials.

Additional issues with hazardous materials include the fact that many materials are hazardous to some people, given allergies to specific materials and combined materials, but not to others.

Other Man-Made Events: Explosions, Facilities Incidents, Theft and Vandalism, and Technology Destruction and Recovery

Explosions

Typically explosions are caused by other emergency activities and events such as fires, earthquakes, and hazardous materials; however, terrorism activities are also the cause of explosions. Prevention is an important part of mitigating and preventing explosions caused by natural situations or as related to other issues, such as fires or earthquakes. Guidelines for hazardous materials also relate to explosions. Specific information about dealing with explosions is found in federal online homeland defense and emergency management content.

Facilities Incidents

Institutions, while following safety standards, can easily suffer internal accidents from age, misuse, construction issues during repair, or human intervention, such as individuals toppling structures either through work-related accidents or constituent use or misuse of materials.

Although these situations are often not included in disaster plans or in emergency management content and are simply accidents, the magnitude of the event, the involvement of employees and/or constituents, and the seriousness of the accident and the presence of injury should dictate whether or not the event warrants an emergency management or disaster planning approach.

For this category—as with the others—insurance issues and the need to document the situation and the following safety and recovery policies and procedures are critical elements of recovery.

Theft and Vandalism

In growing numbers, "theft and vandalism" are being integrated into emergency management and disaster planning due to the increasing frequency and seriousness of events and activities. As with other areas, prevention activities are the focus for institutions with recommendations for policies and procedures, security and/or police, facilities design and management with floor plan designs and vandalism-proof building materials, lighting, signage, and employee and constituent education and training. In addition, marketing and public relations for constituents is an important element informing the public of tolerance levels, policing facilities, and the role of security and police.

Additional recommendations can include security mirrors, security cameras, radio frequency identification (RFID) systems, and other security measures for tagging items. Along with prevention, this area requires extensive training and education for public service employees whose job it is to confront and deal with conflict. Institutions are also recommended to tap into association guidelines and standards on handling theft and vandalism.

Technology Destruction and Recovery

Although this monograph does not specifically address technology nor data loss and recovery, these situations are a growing area of concern. This area of emergency management and disaster planning focuses on prevention on the part of the institution (including duplication and off-site storage), recommends extensive documentation of events and activities, and often outsources recovery to technology experts. The most information on data destruction, loss, and recovery is found in emergency management business continuity content. While there are thousands of data recovery sites on the web, the majority are commercial or sales environments. Institutional technology staff should begin gathering network, systems, and data recovery from the vendors of institutional systems.

EMERGENCY COMMUNICATION POLICIES, PROCEDURES AND PROCESSES, AND SYSTEMS RECOVERY

Because effective communication is considered one of the most important aspects of the management and recovery of disasters and emergencies, entire monographs have been written about communication policies, procedures, and processes, and the role of communication in prevention, mitigation, planning, management, and recovery.

The best approaches to communication include diverse methods, such as print, online, and newer processes that includes texting and broad communication to employees and volunteers, constituents, supporters, and partners as well as systems within buildings. Examples of these systems include standard uses of processes and products, print signage (both temporary and permanent systems), message boards, silent and sound alarms, use of walkie-talkies and other wireless two-way communication systems, public announcement systems, and phone trees.

Disaster Teams/Emergency Management Teams/Process Owners

Managers, employees, volunteers, and community peers and partners play a number of roles and have varied responsibilities in emergency management and disaster recovery processes. These people can exist within the environment identified, carrying out tasks as individuals or team leaders, or as part of a group or team. Roles and responsibilities can include varied competencies (knowledge, skills/abilities, and attitudes) in general and specific areas.

Knowledge

- General safety and security include public safety
- Emergency management and disaster recovery as a discipline
- Continuing education and training curriculum
- Laws, codes, regulations, standards, and guidelines
- Hardware/equipment/technology systems

- Communication, public relations, media background, and critical issues
- Community partnership opportunities

Skills/Abilities

- Delivering continuing education and training
- Applying of laws, codes, regulations, standards, and guidelines
- Using/applying hardware/equipment/technology and software
- Delivering and responding to communication, public relations, and media, both internally and externally
- Technical writing

Attitudes

- Commitment to the emergency management and disaster recovery process
- Enthusiasm for leadership of emergency management and disaster recovery individuals and/or teams and community partners

Appendices

Disaster plan appendices are as varied as the institutions that author them. Typical elements in plans include:

- Assessment/data gathering forms/evaluations
- Budget categories
- Communication plan
- Distribution plan for disaster plan
- Equipment inspection data
- Evacuation plans
- Facilities
- Floor plans

CHAPTER FOUR

- Forms
- Historical information/lessons learned
- Insurance
- Legal issues
- Priorities list with details
- Recovery formulas
- Salvage content and processes
- Schedules
- Supplies
- Surveys
- Time lines
- Technology
- Training materials
- Vendor information
- Weather procedures

CHOOSING DISASTER PLANNING RESOURCES

Emergency Management and Disaster Recovery Supplies

Identifying, purchasing, and managing supplies needed for emergencies and disasters has always been a critical part of the emergency management and disaster recovery program.

Identifying Supplies

- Listing all locations that need supplies
- Listing all functions within locations that need supplies
- Listing all target audiences that will or may need supplies
- Identifying best practices lists from plans of similar institutions or organizations
- Comparing best practices lists against institutional needs

Purchasing Supplies

- Identifying budget categories for acquiring/purchasing supplies
- Identifying categories of both unique supplies needed and general, operational supplies
- Creating purchasing lists based on best practices and institutional assessment
- Consulting emergency management and disaster recovery supply catalogs for unique needs (materials, resources, formats, etc.)
- Consulting emergency management and disaster recovery supply catalogs for general needs

Managing Supplies

- Insuring organizational dollars are available through appropriate budget categories
- Selecting and designing plans for purchasing supplies through standing orders, operating processes, and short-term and long-term plans
- Labeling supply storage locations
- Insuring supplies are placed in operating, short-term and long-term strategic plans
- Labeling supplies (title, contents, use, and date/time stamps)
- Establishing process owners of supply lists by location (including before, during, and after supply deployment)
- Creating sign in/sign out usage sheets for supply storage locations
- Creating sign in/sign out usage sheets for individual supplies in storage locations
- Creating and locating inventory lists of supplies in locations
- Identifying, posting, and labeling any unique storage re-

quirements (bottles on sides, temperature, kit items being
kept together or apart, danger postings)
- Gathering special issues concerning supply packaging issues, including allergies, shelf-life, chemical combinations,
and reactions to substances
- Identifying training issues related to supplies
- Identifying institutional documents needing supply informa-
tion, such as job descriptions, job advertisements, assessments and evaluations, budgets, and training materials
- Disseminating training material information to training/con-
tinuing education process owners
- Submitting process owner responsibility information for ad-
ditions to institutional documents
- Establishing assessment processes for supply locations
- Establishing time lines for maintaining and updating supply
inventory lists
- Creating floor plans of supply inventory locations
- Designing notification (and, as needed, communication)
plans for supply processes
- Designing supply list forms by emergency for grant applica-
tions
- Designing supply list forms by emergency for consultant/ex-
pert contracts
- Designing supply list forms by emergency for inclusion with
documentation and reporting out (umbrella agencies, peers,
partners, annual reports, etc.)

Although best practices plans and recommended websites identify dozens of critical supplies, there are also recommended
general categories of supplies that are arranged by event or activity, such as emergency weather supplies and/or natural disaster
supplies; first aid supplies, general medical supplies; (nonprescrip-
tion); supply category including tools, equipment; audience—

employee and/or constituent, such as clothing, food/nutrition/
kitchen, and comfort resources; and support/documentation.
Extensive supply lists and examples of supplies needed for general disaster recovery and emergency management can be found in
several locations including the Federal Emergency Management
Agency and Homeland Security websites. Subcategories of general
supply categories (type of event and activity) typically include
tools, equipment (fasteners, pumps, hoses, sandbags, energy gen-
erators, and energy support materials, such as batteries), fuel,
lighting, medical, clothing, bedding, sanitation and hygiene needs
(purchase and rental), office supplies, reporting/documentation
(cameras and video), institutional money, construction/building
materials, food/nutrition and food preparation resources, comfort
items (recreational materials, reading materials, and toys), and individual information, such as individual money, duplicate keys,
multiple identification forms of critical documents, lists of account
numbers/passwords, emergency contact lists, and area maps.

Extensive supply lists and examples of supplies needed for
unique materials for disaster recovery and emergency management can be in several locations including bibliographic networks,
the Library of Congress, and the National Archives. Under typical
general categories, such as emergency or disaster event or activity,
are subcategories of unique supply categories such as materials
and resources for books, serials, audiovisuals (for example, films),
photographs, realia, and works of art such as sculpture. Additional
subcategories are type of damage such as water, fire, and mold including treatment of damage: air drying, antimicrobial, blast freezing, dehumidification, deodorization, disinfectant, freezing and
freeze drying, HEPA filter, mold and mildew, ozone, refrigeration
(storage and transportation), smoke/soot, and sterilization.

The number of vendors and vendor locations (catalog and web)
for acquiring supplies has increased dramatically in the last decade
and although unique supplies (conservation and preservation for
materials and resources) can be found in unique locations, several

vendor sources are available and considered extensive resource locations. In addition, supplies can now be purchased separately or supply-by-supply, through the purchase of kits assembly by type of emergency (a "hurricane kit"), or kits by recovery (a "wet book" kit).

Tips for Managing Supplies

- Create dynamic processes for storing supplies. Supplies stored away from frequent view are quickly forgotten.
- Establish immediate training for deploying supplies to all levels and types of employees including, as appropriate, volunteers.
- Establish checks and balances for monitoring supply-by-supply use. First aid kits typically come with usage forms, and these forms—or altered forms to meet your specific needs—should be monitored on a standard, frequent schedule.
- Consider dividing supplies into "likely" and "less than likely" to be used and labeling and storing them accordingly. That is, a first aid kit is likely to be used often, while a medical emergency kit is not. "Do not cross" banners from a safety kit are more likely to be used than safety flares.
- Document the environment *before* the disaster or emergency occurs. That is, create a "before" scrapbook of all areas of the environment for comparing and contrasting the "before" pictures with "after" pictures for more accurate damage and recovery estimates for using supplies. Create multiple copies of "before" content and store off-site.
- Plan specific, consistent meetings and visits with partners before disasters and emergencies to share recovery information specific to resources and supplies.
- Establish relationships (invite on-site) with supply vendors prior to disasters and emergencies so vendors will have knowledge of the institution and institutional needs.

BEST PRACTICES: DISASTER PLANS

Examples such as selecting the best disaster plan, the most relevant scenarios to use in training, or a process for cleaning print materials infested with mold includes the process of gathering information and matching it to your needs. A process for this match is—in today's professional literature—the process for choosing a best practice to use.

Best practices are defined in a wide variety of ways and can include the selection of processes, practices, organizations, or documents that have won awards; choosing a standard way of doing business based on, for example, an association standard of behavior or design; the choice of processes used by organizations identified as "sister" organizations (usually by umbrella organizations); or the choice of practices touted as examples of product or performance excellence by consultants or experts.

In identifying best practices, elements are reviewed for assessment and comparison.

The following characteristics are identified as present, in some degree and mostly in part, in best practice settings.

Assessment

- Significant measurement and assessment has taken place to provide organizations with information on data related to the content area in question or overall assessment of performance.
- Significant measurement and assessment has taken place to provide organizations with information on data related to use of the organization's resources and services.
- Significant measurement and assessment has taken place to provide organizations with information on data related to an overall profile of the organization, including strengths, weaknesses, opportunities, and threats.
- Significant measurement and assessment has taken place to

provide organizations with information on data related to an overall profile of the organization's umbrella structure, activities, and support.

• Significant measurement and assessment has taken place to provide organizations with information on data related to an overall profile of the organization's "community."

Communication

• The organization is committed to open, accurate, and continuously improved communication through verbal and written general communication as well as documents that include things like marketing, publication relations information, and plans such as budgets, long-range plans, operational goals, and the like.

• Upon scrutiny, employees indicate that significant, positive interpersonal communications occur.

Organizational Structure

• The organizational structure provides a successful infrastructure for carrying out primary vision and goals and provides a structure for supporting risks, new ideas, and change in general.

Management

• Managers have identified management policies and practices for managing performance and organizing workload, managing conflicts, providing a structure for employees to work alone or through workgroups and/or teams, managing conflict, putting systems and procedures in place for solving problems and focusing on motivating employees.

Leadership

- Leadership activities include establishing and building commitment to a vision for the organization as a whole as well as for goals and practices.
- The organization identifies leadership as a priority and focuses on mentoring for both individuals and teams for general professional development as well as for the organization's projects and products.
- Leadership takes an active role in addressing change.

Continuous Learning/Development

- The organization provides content and opportunities for professional growth, related personal growth, basic competency development, and advanced and unique competency development (where appropriate).

Other benchmark quality elements include value of diversity, excellence in customer satisfaction, employee satisfaction, revenue/profit margins (if applicable), economy and/or efficiency (if applicable), partnerships and collaboration, existence of creativity and innovation, and a commitment to and passion for the profession.

5

INTEGRATING EMERGENCY/ DISASTER PLANNING INTO THE ORGANIZATION

CONTENTS

- Scenario: Orientation, Training, and Education
- Integrating Emergency/Disaster Planning into Libraries
- Integrating the Disaster Plan
- Staff Development: Training, Continuing Education, and Professional Development
- Working with Stakeholders

INTEGRATING EMERGENCY/DISASTER PLANNING INTO THE ORGANIZATION

SCENARIO: ORIENTATION, TRAINING, AND EDUCATION

June Carter was scheduled to advertise her reference librarian's position when the new budget year began. Because this position replaced a retiring librarian *and* because it was the first new hire in the last five years, June was taking her time preparing the documents for the process and the organization.

First she gathered all organizational documents dealing with personnel and then reviewed elements of the job description, the position advertisement, and the position evaluation form. Additionally, she gathered documents used to train new employees and discovered her documents were woefully out of date. The only recent new employees were hourly staff and therefore had out-of-date first day/ first week and first month orientation, first year/job specific training, and short-term continuing education and professional development plans. Although June took the responsibility of reviewing and revising the job description and job ad, she contacted the training team and charged them with assessing needs for the orientation, training, and continuing education updates.

The training team reviewed the documents by assessing the last five years of annual reports to determine what had changed in the organization. Major initiatives were identified and then assessed for possible impact and additions to documents related to a reference librarian's position. Reports and other documents revealed a number of areas that would have to be integrated into job content as well as orientation, training, and continuing education. These areas included such issues as the emergency management and disaster recovery planning that had been the focus of the last three years.

Upon review of the content, information sorted into resources for the new librarian included:

- Addition of roles and responsibilities to the job description
- Addition of competency areas to the job description
- Addition of content into the job advertisement
- Content inserted into first day/first week orientation
- Content added to training materials
- Content added to continuing education

Examples of emergency management and disaster recovery content in these areas included:

- Addition of roles and responsibilities to the job description
  - Possibility of process ownership
  - Possibility of backup to facility management
- Addition of competency areas to the job description
  - Knowledge of general emergency management and disaster recovery issues
  - Ability to assist constituents with special needs in emergency management and disaster events and activities
  - Commitment to integrating processes into institutional operations
- Addition of content into the job advertisement
  - Basic knowledge statement
  - Basic commitment statement
- Content inserted into first day/first week orientation
  - Safety and security issues for employees
  - Safety and security issues for constituents
  - Required training
  - Awareness of the major documentation
  - Knowledge of locations of basic equipment and supplies

- o Knowledge of storage and access points for critical supplies
- o Awareness of recordkeeping critical to assessment
- Content added to training materials
  - o In-depth review of the disaster plan
  - o Training in process ownership areas
  - o Training in assisting constituents and employees
  - o Knowledge of media/public relation issues
  - o Knowledge of and ability to use safety and security equipment and hardware
- Content added to continuing education
  - o Leadership development for leading teams and partners
  - o Project management coursework

June asked the training team to vet content against the reference librarians to see if where content was placed was appropriate and requested human resources to ensure there was a match of content to the job description and evaluation. As a final reality check, June contacted the area library association for advice on the newest orientation and training techniques.

INTEGRATING EMERGENCY/DISASTER PLANNING INTO LIBRARIES

Although there are general and specific issues applicable to all types of libraries, there are unique aspects for emergency management and disaster recovery in libraries. These are often *not* exclusive to one type of library but instead contain ways to treat issues identified in all types of libraries.

Academic Libraries

- Umbrella institutions may have more content specific to and required for the library.

- Recovery plans have more content on issues related to diverse formats as well as unique and rare materials.
- Extended facilities and service hours necessitate specific evacuation and constituent support information.
- Unique materials and resources necessitate expanded budget areas.
- Selection of a trainer with appropriate experience/curriculum is required.
- Training is required for unique aspects.

Public Libraries

- Constituent issues include more diverse situations for communication, given public library constituent age ranges.
- Constituents may have more special issues for evacuations (e.g., older Americans and young children).
- Umbrella institution disaster plans are primarily good general guides but more content can be used specifically for the library.
- External partnerships are critical relationships for all stages of emergency management and disaster recovery.
- Local or regional content materials and resources often qualify as rare and unique.
- Selection of a trainer with appropriate experience/curriculum is necessary.
- Training is required for unique aspects.

School Libraries

- Umbrella institutions have very content-specific emergency management and disaster recovery for school libraries, and typically fewer additions need to be made to create plans specific to school libraries.
- Internal partnerships are critical parts of school library plans.

- Budgets are as extensive for recovery of school library materials; however, dollars may not be available at the building level but instead at the umbrella institution or district level.
- Selection of a trainer with appropriate experience/curriculum is necessary.
- Training is required for unique aspects.

Special Libraries

- Recovery of materials is at issue as much of the special library data is proprietary information.
- Partnerships may not be available due to the content/proprietary nature of data.
- Many disaster plans from umbrella institutions do not provide content closely applicable to special libraries, and plans must be created from other best practice special library plans.
- Selection of a trainer with appropriate experience/curriculum is necessary.
- Training is required for unique aspects.

INTEGRATING THE DISASTER PLAN

Once the disaster plan has been designed for the institution, administrators and managers must integrate it into the practices of the institution and any/all umbrella organization areas and community and partnership environments. As a management document, the plan must stand alone, but it must also be integrated by extrapolating content for related documents; adding policies and processes to existing documents; designing communication tools, such as media/public relations issues based on plan content; integrating content into partnership documents, such as contracts, agreements, vision, and values statements, general plans, and budgets; and, repurposing content for items such as grants and/or training curriculum.

Administrators and managers should work with the team that wrote the document to determine all venues for integrating content after the document has been accepted and/or approved as the organization's disaster plan. Recommendations for integration include the following.

- Integrate information as quickly as possible not only for the importance of content but also to communicate the organization's serious commitment to emergency management and disaster recovery issues.
- Establish an integration checklist to ensure that all documents and resources populated with plan information are updated as the plan is updated.
- Make a distinct effort to get approval and/or "sign off" on all partnership environments to be able to integrate plan content into all relevant partnership documents.
- "Announce" or publicize the creation/approval of the plan to communicate its importance to the widest possible audience.

STAFF DEVELOPMENT: TRAINING, CONTINUING EDUCATION, AND PROFESSIONAL DEVELOPMENT

One of the most important aspects of the emergency management and disaster recovery process—after the design and general distribution of the plan—is the design of curriculum and the delivery of that curriculum into the "life" of the institution. The "Scenario: Orientation, Training, and Education" section that introduced this chapter illustrated the need for the widest possible interpretation of "need to know" for emergency management and disaster recovery materials. The following documents from the scenario serve as a base for institutional success if integrated into documents and curriculum and include (in order of mention):

- Reference librarian's position description, including roles and responsibilities (articulates basic curriculum needed for most employees)
- Position advertisement, including competency areas and content (articulates basic curriculum needed for most employees)
- Position evaluation forms responsibilities (articulates basic curriculum needed for most employees)
- First day orientation (required curriculum)
- First week orientation (required curriculum)
- First month orientation (required and recommended curriculum)
- First year/job specific training (required and recommended curriculum)
- Short-term continuing education (required and recommended curriculum)
- Professional development plans (required and recommended curriculum)
- Training team needs assessment (required and recommended curriculum)
- Annual reports (assessment, communication curriculum)
- Safety and security content for employees and constituents (required curriculum)
- Inventory, including basic equipment and basic supplies (required curriculum)
- Inventory, including advanced equipment and advanced supplies (advanced, recommended curriculum)
- Floor plans, including evacuation and storage (required curriculum)
- Data gathering/recordkeeping forms (required curriculum)
- Assessment statements, including goals and outcomes (recommended curriculum)

- Media/public relations issues (advanced, recommended curriculum)
- Management and leadership development content (advanced, recommended curriculum)
- Project management coursework (advanced, recommended curriculum)

While not all of these documents are specific to training at first glance, all documents should be used throughout an effective emergency management and disaster recovery curriculum. In addition to the content specifically used to illustrate or convey emergency management and disaster recovery information, orientation, training, and continuing education and professional development issues related to this specific training include the following areas:

Teaching Styles/Techniques Specific to This Curriculum

Active learning, interactive learning, case method, and scenario teaching techniques are styles that are successful with content best learned through practical application. These techniques provide context and a frame of reference that can be unique to institutions and institutional needs and—because context is articulated—are faster ways of presenting and learning these critical issues.

Learning Styles Specific to This Curriculum

Those needing orientation, training, and continuing education and professional development should be assessed to determine how they learn critical information as well as how they learn basic important content most quickly.

Assessment Issues Specific to This Curriculum

Because some content is basic and required, assessing who has learned what and who can apply the information is a critical part of the orientation and training process. In addition, those being assessed can benefit from pre- and post-testing to provide data in the absence of baseline data as well as for comparison data. Unlike other training areas, if emergencies or disaster events or activities occur, consulting training materials may *not* be the most expedient way of performing basic, required tasks or responsibilities (such as basic evacuation, and/or special needs evaluation, etc.).

Two additional important aspects of orientation, training, and continuing education include *who* manages the diverse curriculum delivery (amid the variety of other content delivery that must take place in library and information settings) and *who* assumes responsibility for basic and advanced content.

- **Resident experts**: Staff who have been identified as knowledgeable or potentially knowledgeable in an area of emergency management or disaster recovery and do not teach, present, or do workshops, instead are "on call" to answer questions, give advice, or participate in management events or activities. Resident experts in institutions produce training materials, FAQs, tip sheets, instructions, and handouts and have unique competencies. They may also be assigned to handle or manage one particular area of the process, such as gathering data and/or data assessment.
- **Training/continuing education /professional development specialists**: These positions typically have all or a major part of their job designated for emergency management and disaster recovery training. These individuals teach, train, educate, develop, plan, coordinate, and present information; assess, track, measure, report on, and communicate learning outcomes; and work with resident experts and other content specialists.
- **Staff development team or committee or work group**: Teams meet and review data, advise on assessment and direction, assist in curriculum management including evaluation

and assigning, project future trends, and divide up activities as well as seek institutional expertise.

- **Train the trainer**: Although this is typically seen as a process instead of a position, this *can* be seen as a function of someone on staff. This person's job is to specialize in preparing other staff for either one-on-one or group roles in instruction and assistance. A "train-the-trainer" works with the team or committee to determine which content to learn and repurpose as well as recommend individuals for further training. He/she often has teaching experience, specifically in adult teaching and learning.
- **Peer training**: Peer training identifies individuals to partner or team with other individuals within the organization. These peer relationships offer opportunities for self-directed or small group study following training, observation for practical application, and—where needed—interpretation for partners.

If organizations do choose one or some of the above positions or if they don't choose to identify and define multistaff levels (too small, not enough expertise, little training money), at the very least they should identify resident/content experts and peer training opportunities.

For example, a small library might have a content expert to whom they can turn for review of technical instructions used in training their staff. This person might look at workshop content or review the agenda of a conference to determine which programs might benefit the organization and which ones a staff member might report back on.

WORKING WITH STAKEHOLDERS

Identifying or establishing profiles for existing umbrella institution or community stakeholders is the first step in identifying and integrating partners for both formal and informal relationships of emergency management and disaster recovery events and activities. Stakeholder profiles should be articulated, stakeholder contact information should be located, and strategies for reaching and interesting stakeholders should be determined. Profiles of stakeholders include a determination of how they communicate, when they communicate, the best match of stakeholder to institution, opportunities for stakeholder feedback, and criteria for moving stakeholders from stakeholder relationships to partnership relationships.

Planning Partnerships, Both Internal and External

Partnerships

Many library environments assess stakeholders in the community or environment to determine possibilities for more significant relationships and then enter into partnerships, collaboratives, consortia, and shared or joint use environments. Although these settings range from very successful to moderately successful (and some not successful at all), the model is here to stay. When dealing with all library and information issues and with the broad universe of emergency management issues, library administrators and managers must address various rules, regulations, policies, procedures, and other issues that are part of successfully handling these issues. In addition, it is critical that librarians educate their umbrella organizations, governing and advisory groups, institutions, and employees about these relationships as well as which elements might need to be included in initial agreement statements and/or contracts entered into by participating organizations.

In general, these areas include:

- The assignment and placement within the organizational structure of both organizations with those individuals responsible for emergency management issues related to the partnership

- The inclusion of language that focuses on outcomes for the "end user" or patron or client in vision, mission, and goals statements.
- Content unique to partners integrated into scenarios and cases
- The inclusion of partners, specifically employees and constituents, in strategic planning projects
- A communication plan that includes all partners
- Time lines that include all partnership issues for planning, implementation, and maintenance
- Content for partners integrated into business plans, marketing plans, and technology plans
- Design of training and continuing education materials integrating partnerships

Examples of partnerships where issues exist include but are not limited to the following scenarios.

Public library environments provide space for ongoing meeting and training space for community organizations without accommodations of their own. Likely partners for public libraries seeking space to conduct business include family organizations that exist to offer social services to families. These include conflict resolution organizations and social service programs for victims of domestic violence. Safety and security (emergency) issues relating to meeting participants or workshop attendees could include attacks on committee or work group members or workshop students at the public library. Emergency management and disaster recovery issues could include communication issues between the institution and the organization regarding notification of *potential* problems, the nature of procedures to alert law enforcement officials, and processes for evacuating public library patrons versus processes for evacuating partner organization environments.

Academic libraries partner with area high schools to bring high school students/classes into campus libraries for instruction in information literacy and college-level research, among other services. Campus violence against campus constituents provides partners with the need to articulate behavior in areas such as managing underage constituents in emergency situations and notifying families and health care professionals of underage campus constituents as victims.

Emergency management and disaster recovery safety and security issues must be addressed for partnerships at the local, regional, state, and national levels that offer shared costs and delivery of specialized access to constituents of school, public, and academic libraries. These issues must include addressing compromising networks for hacking into user data as well as hacking into commercial content delivered. Additional issues include the critical need for establishing policies, procedures, and budget issues relating to remote storage of data among environments to provide safe havens in the event of catastrophic events destroying partner information.

School library and public library joint use, contiguous, and/or shared buildings necessitate an extensive assessment of legislation, city and county codes, school district rules, regulations and policies, and state education code assessment to design partnership and contractual agreements as well as new legal and social infrastructure for required and recommended administration and management for the partnership. Emergency content must be included in all partnership language and documentation to provide information on safety and security for all ages of constituents working and using open or public environments as well as information for shared technology and combined personal and usage data on school and public library users.

Are you involved in partnerships, either formal or informal, that would necessitate addition of emergency management content? Specifically:

- Is there a genuine commitment to partners articulating (both general and emergency management) issues relating to both organizations?
- Are personnel in both organizations identified as key resource people to plan, implement, and maintain emergency mitigation and response action plans?
- Does the partnership have a written articulation that includes emergency management content?
- Is data, which has been gathered and stored, assessed for safety and security issues including multiple storage environments and are there plans to mitigate hacking and electronic theft of content?
- Are institutional time lines reviewed to design reasonable layout, implementation, and maintenance of emergency management action plans?
- Are emergency management employees, processes, and activities integrated into organizational assessment and outcomes assessment?
- Do all organizational budgets include dollars for supporting emergency management activities and issues?

Planning for/Partnering with the Media

Planning for communicating with the media and other groups is an ongoing process within institutions; however, informing them during emergency management and disaster recovery is a complicated process that requires expertise, concern for timeliness, standardization of policies and processes, and before, during, and after events or activities. In order to best communicate events and activities, communications plan elements should be integrated into general communication policies and processes, and if a general communication plan does *not* exist, a plan specific to emergency management and disaster recovery should be developed. These plans provide standards and guidelines for communicating within the institution and between and among umbrella institutional partners and the general community, including from the institution to the media and constituents.

Typically these plans provide job descriptions, roles, and responsibilities and describe the role of institutional media representatives in communicating general, specific, and critical information regarding emergency management and disaster recovery information. Although a variety of plans are identified in appendix A, basic plan elements include:

- The seriousness of the event/activity and whether or not the situation warrants use of the communications plan
- Implementing plan actions, including informing appropriate constituencies, gathering and communicating facts, answering critical questions, minimizing incorrect information, and assisting in recovery
- Assembling the institution's individuals and groups trained to assist during events and activities.

Roles and Responsibilities of Communications Individuals and Work Groups

Individuals and groups involved in the institution's emergency management and disaster recovery communication activities include:

- Resident experts who serve as content experts regarding facilities, activities, materials, or resources
- Communications director/media relations individuals whose primary responsibility is communication and media in general as well as unique situations, such as emergency management and disaster recovery

- Police and/or security
- Network/computing and communications
- Highest level administrator and/or manager
- Management in charge of a facility
- Constituent groups such as friends member, foundation staff or board members, parent groups, and governing/advisory board members

Items to include in the communications include:

- Institutional data/facts relating to issues such as facilities data, collection size, square feet of building
- Fact sheets (to be completed per event/activity)
- Media contact information
  - General media
  - Unique media outlets (first responders, such as police and fire squads)
- Media processes (appropriate to the event/activity)
- Communication/media assessment per event/activity as well as the communication plan
- appendices
  - Institutional communication designees contact information
  - Communication tool
  - Sample media/communication pieces
  - Preferred communication channels per event/activity
- Communication tips

6

DAY ONE/ DAY OF: RESPONDING TO EMERGENCY/ DISASTER EVENTS, BOTH INTERNAL AND EXTERNAL

CONTENTS

6

DAY ONE/DAY OF: RESPONDING TO EMERGENCY/DISASTER EVENTS, BOTH INTERNAL AND EXTERNAL

SCENARIO: DAY ONE RESPONSES TO EMERGENCIES

In the first few minutes of a Wednesday business day, Mark was startled to hear a loud explosion while sitting in his director's office. He grabbed his orange emergency/disaster jacket, his cell phone, the institution's walkie-talkie, the digital camera, and his megaphone and ran out of his office toward the noise to the north of the building and found a car burning in the back parking lot of the library.

He immediately used his megaphone to clear the parking lot, called 911 on the cell phone, and then used the walkie-talkie to contact the floor leader to direct a building evacuation to the south side of the building and to start the communication/phone tree. Using the digital camera, he took pictures of the explosion area as well as the area surrounding the accident to indicate the isolated nature of the destruction.

The building was evacuated by other facility managers, Mark called the director of communications, texted his supervisor Bev, and kept constituents out of the north lot using the institution's emergency kit with traffic cones, tape, and flares. When first responders arrived (police, fire, and EMS), he then directed them through the lots in front of the building to the north lot.

While Mark worked outside answering questions, directing constituents, answering questions from first responders, and taking pic-

tures, managers and process owners worked inside to carry out disaster plan processes to:
- Identify, protect, and direct constituents
- Secure the environment
- Carry out communication plan elements by:
  - Addressing upcoming events planned for the day by contacting participants
  - Addressing upcoming events by posting signage
- Communicate with library management on activities
- Support first responders

When the explosion was contained, Mark worked with explosion scene individuals to clarify/identify the incident as accident-related, rather than terrorism, civil disobedience, or vandalism. When the environment was cleaned, the automobile towed, and the parking lot cleared for reentry, Mark moved back inside, pulled together his managers and process owners for a quick meeting and reviewed the situation and necessary paperwork that needed completing. Following the update from staff and the assignment to complete paperwork online, Mark e-mailed links to completed online paperwork, e-mailed the digital images from the morning for Bev to share with other administrators and the communications director as she saw fit, and set up a Skype discussion with the communications director and his supervisor Bev as a Day One post-event update and assessment.

DAY ONE ELEMENTS

In assessing event/activity issues Mark reviewed:

- "Rolling out" emergency/disaster documents
- Safety for staff (general and special needs)
- Safety for customers (general and special needs)
- Communication—internal

Assessment questions included:

- Did disaster plan content cover the accident event activity for accident scene activities?
- Did disaster plan content cover the accident event activity for nonaccident scene activities?
- Did staff managers fulfill roles and responsibilities based on plan job descriptions?
- Did staff process owners fulfill roles and responsibilities based on plan job descriptions?
- Did forms for identifying patrons meet needs?
- Did evacuation plans meet needs (guidelines for evacuating and floor plans)?
- Did emergency kit supplies meet needs (event scene identification and first aid kit)?
- Did archived signs meet all needs for labeling the environment?
- Did communication processes meet needs?
  - Phone/contact tree?
  - Text messages to upper-level supervisors?
  - Contacts with communications director?
  - Skype meeting post-event activity?
- Were the digital pictures clear?

HUMAN ISSUES FOR ASSISTING STAFF AND CONSTITUENTS IN DEALING WITH EMERGENCIES/DISASTERS

Most emergency management plans and disaster recovery documents have extensive content on managing facilities, collections, and resources as well as how to move constituents to safety, identify and track constituents, and manage staff involved and ancillary to the process. However, the reality is that the mental or emotional issues of the effects of emergencies and disasters are dealt with but seldom codified or "planned for."

And if standard treatment and concerns *are* identified for employees, volunteers, and partners, there are related issues that need attention, such as illness (prolonged) and death (sudden/accidental). Sadly disaster plans must now be revised to include stress, illness, and death-related incidents from violence within the workplace and on campus.

Although it is impossible to predict many elements of all emergencies and disasters, the human element, either as perpetrators or victims, can be addressed before, during, and after events. There are plans that can be made and steps that can be taken in advance of events to insure additional safety and security of constituents and staff and to insure a positive organizational response. Existing documents and how they might be revised include:

Communication Plan

Communication plans must take broad approaches to outlining responsibilities and empowering staff with procedures and content dealing with the human side of situations. Many organizations have one general communication plan with integrated content while others have separate plans for human issues involving staff, volunteers, and constituents.

A major aspect of this additional information is that content must approach the institution from a 24/7 perspective; that is, what happens during open hours as well as during regularly closed hours, vacation/holiday, and emergency closed hours. Dealing with the situation during work hours and informing workers of issues/ situations prior to coming to work insures efficient and effective communication.

Communication plans should address political correctness of communication and content, disability access, religious issues, language, literacy levels, and both formal and informal communication including dealing with facts and rumors with special care taken to follow legal/government guidelines, such as HIPAA legislation. In several types of libraries, worker and worker family content consideration must be given to design and delivery of content for a wide variety of age levels.

Building/Library Evacuation Plan of Action

Great attention must be given to "before" activities that serve to provide secure feelings for workers, including attention to evacuation policies and procedures, training on safety, training on dealing with health issues, and support mechanisms in place for assisting workers in recovery.

Other Staff Support Issues

While personal conflicts or tragedy situations are certainly not new in the workplace, they have the potential of occurring more often. Managers must outline what the organizational policies are, what procedures are in effect, and what the options are for problems/situations. While some events and activities are bigger than the institution and might be local, state, regional, and/or national, others may be unique to the organization (a staff member or family member is dying or has been killed) and need to be addressed as carefully. Recommended approaches include:

- Act quickly and keep in touch with individuals involved.
- Refer staff to other professionals/sources as needed.
- Identify worker responsibilities.

Act quickly. Managers should address issues immediately. This can include doing nothing more than immediately sending a communiqué initially recognizing that the event(s) has occurred, management's concern for the situation and for workers, identifying whom to speak with, and clarifying lines of communication.

Keep in touch. Managers should acknowledge the situation and worker support and continue to monitor the situation.

Refer staff to other professionals/sources as needed. Managers should clarify support resources available and keep staff aware of other resources, such as print or online support material. Managers should identify workers who need to be "walked" somewhere or directed toward help and decide whether or not they need to bring counselors or other professionals *in* to the organization to assist workers in their recovery.

Identify worker responsibilities. Managers should outline worker responsibilities for accessing content, reading, keeping up to date, and following policies and procedures during situations.

Human Issues for Assisting Customers in Dealing with Emergencies/Disasters

Just as worker and staff mental and emotional issue support is not included in disaster plans, most "dealing with tragedy and conflict" constituent information directed to employees or for constituents (signage, instructions, and training) is not included in disaster plans. Plans should address how the public should interact during all stages of these difficult times and should contain specific examples and scenarios of what staff should say, what they should not say, and how they should interact during all aspects of the situation. Special care should be taken to outline how staff should talk to *each other* during these times as both constituents and staff members may be directly affected by events or activities.

7

DAY TWO AND BEYOND

CONTENTS

- Scenario: Post-emergency
- Documenting Emergency Management and Disaster Recovery
- Assessment

DAY TWO AND BEYOND

SCENARIO: POST-EMERGENCY

First thing Thursday morning following the Wednesday morning explosion, Mark parked in the back of the library and perused the parking lot to ensure it was returned to a safe location status. He toured the parking areas in general to make sure all police tape was gone and that the traffic cones, his jacket, and the megaphone had been placed back into emergency management storage. He checked to make sure the walkie-talkies were placed back on chargers and then toured the building to ensure yesterday's signs had been removed. He checked his e-mail and text messages to make sure the director of communications didn't have any more questions and that his boss, Bev, had all she needed to file reports. He reviewed the day two signs for accuracy and asked the floor manager to distribute and post signs so that the public would have current information on the event from the day before. Mark read the newspaper story again to ensure its accuracy and to make sure it dispelled rumors and was clear that the explosion was not a terrorist attack nor workplace violence. He then copied the newspaper story for the circulation and reference staff to give as handouts if asked about the event.

Mark crafted an internal e-mail to reassure staff and to outline the day's activities to assess how the disaster plan "worked" and how the communications processes, such as the phone tree, worked the previous day and how they supported the recovery period as well. Mark asked his boss Bev to attend his a.m. meeting and waited until she arrived to bring everyone together. When the meeting began, Mark passed out completed forms regarding the accident, the phone tree used, the disaster plan with tabs on pages people used the day before, the constituent sign-in list, the signs used on Day One and the signs posted for Day Two and projected the digital images from the accident scene.

During the meeting, staff assessed plan documents and whether or not they felt that staff and constituents felt safe. Mark offered to bring counselors in to the library to discuss any safety concerns. He asked Bev for permission to send his images to first responders on the scene and to ask if it was appropriate to include digital images for the insurance claims regarding cleaning and resurfacing the parking area.

Specific questions he posed to the group included:

- Did the disaster plan meet needs?
- Did staff and process owners fulfill roles and responsibilities based on plan job descriptions?
- Were completed forms appropriate?
- Were there appropriate forms to match all needs for Day One and Day Two?
- Did evacuation plans meet needs?
- Did emergency supplies meet needs? What was used and what needed to be replaced?
- Did emergency signs meet needs from Day One and Day Two?
- Did communication processes meet needs and did all forms of communication work?
- Did the library resume work within a reasonable period of time?

Other "beyond" questions included:

- Did the library resume business in a timely fashion? What business was interrupted and why?
- Did institutional training meet needs for staff security and management expectation?
- Were any health-related issues reported? Smoke issues? First aid used?
- How was the media "handled"?

- Was documentation sufficient to complete the post-event/activity needs?
- How did first responders operate?
- Did first responders arrive in a timely manner?
- Did first responders work in partnership with library staff?
- What additional steps for recovery were needed?
- What outstanding issues existed?
- How were personal issues that inhibited business recovery needs addressed?
- Was public perception handled appropriately?
- Would outside vendors be needed for recovery?
- Were there any cleanup regulatory issues, such as cleanup of hazardous materials? Any special permits required?
- Were there any follow-up issues regarding constituents?

DOCUMENTING EMERGENCY MANAGEMENT AND DISASTER RECOVERY

Documenting events and activities and responses to them is a critical part of emergency management and disaster recovery. Documenting the environment of the institution includes "before" documentation and data-gathering, "during" documentation and data-gathering, and "after" documentation and data-gathering. Individuals can document with regular cameras, digital cameras, camera phones, voice recorders, and video recorders; however, the institution should decide on standards for documentation and adhere to those in policies and procedures as well as in training.

"Before" documentation and data-gathering includes:

- Photographing the environment to establish context and frame of reference

- Duplicating emergency management and disaster recovery print contents
- Duplicating emergency management and disaster recovery web content by downloading/burning to media
- Duplicating and storing data in remote locations
- Purchasing multiple info tech appliances for creating duplicate images
- Training employees to create documentation
- Training employees on data-gathering and assessment
- Identifying process owners for documentation
- Archiving content

"During" documentation and data-gathering includes:

- Time lines and schedules for process owners to document during the activity
- Safety guidelines, event-by-event, for documentation by process owners
- Establishing context and frame of reference by using scale images to indicate size and magnitude of documented items/environments
- Duplicating and archiving documentation during the event

"After" Documentation and data-gathering includes:

- Creating portfolios of events/activities
- Assessing quality
- Matching documentation to content for management, assessment, and insurance
- Replenishing info tech appliances used in documentation
- Continuous training on documentation and data-gathering

No matter when documentation occurs, a number of recommendations are critical to the success of using documentation and data gathered. They include:

- Those documenting and recording content with digital images need to ask permission for all images pictured of employees and constituents. Permission should be articulated by a permission form with written signatures.
- Documentation should be planned to ensure speed for "during" and "after" events and activities.

ASSESSMENT

Although extensive questions are asked in a number of forums, including the branch meeting on Day Two, data-gathering processes should include:

- Surveys to staff on duty at the library the day of the accident
- Surveys to staff in the library *not* on Day One during the event, but on duty on Day One after the event and on Day Two
- Surveys to media personnel (director of communications and other staff) on handling media coverage during and after the event
- Surveys to constituents in the building during the event
- Surveys to administration (Bev, Mark's boss) on her/their opinions of how the staff operated and the plans worked
- Surveys to Mark for a self-assessment of events/activities and handling of the situations
- A focus group of constituents in the library during the accident
- A focus group of library workers in the library during the accident
- A focus group of managers in the library during the accident
- A focus group of process owners in the library during the accident
- An assessment of digital images taken

- A critique of paperwork reporting and documenting the event/
  activity
- A specific meeting post-assessment with managers to discuss
  "lessons learned" to answer:
  - What would managers do differently?
  - What would process owners do differently?
  - What would library workers do differently?
  - What supplies were missing?
  - What signage was not available/should have been there for
    future events?

Appendix A

RESOURCES

To say there are hundreds of resources on emergency management and disaster recovery, within library and information science, specific emergency management and disaster recovery disciplines, *and* in related areas is an understatement. And although there were quality resources prior to 9/11, all professional literature has expanded so significantly and consistently, that it literally appears to have no end. The literature before and after 9/11 differs dramatically: there is much more content, contexts have changed, the frame of reference often relates to twenty-first-century specific events, there is significant North American content in addition to global content, and the magnitude and recommendations for handling the scale of events and communications are outlined. In addition, the literature includes lessons learned as well as the exponential growth of supporting resources, agencies, services, and experts. Another major change is that there has been great growth for specific organizations such as types of libraries or umbrella organizations. As an example, while there were materials on academic library disasters in the area of resource damage and destruction, today's higher education environment now includes significant "terrorism-like" or small group or individual attacks on the educational environment. While these issues *did* occur earlier (e.g. the 1960s campus revolutions) there is much more "campus under siege" content today. However, there is one major area where new or first-time content exists—K–12 educational campuses, given the Columbine and Amish West Nickel Mines School events.

Identifying content, establishing criteria for inclusion in a bibliography, deciding on which content to include, and annotating resources ended up being the easiest part of data gathering, inclusion, and presentation. The hardest part was the decision on how to organize the resources—if I organized resources other than in alphabetical order—*how* should they be organized and categorized. So, after several attempts at organizing, I chose a simple structure that includes a combination of types of resources, formats, and audience. In addition, sections include an introductory paragraph that provides background on categories to assist readers in deciding what they might choose to read first or to move from a general bibliography to a manager's actual or digital "bookshelf."

Finally, although a few media resources are included under "Miscellaneous," items such as videos, CD-ROMs, and DVD's were not included because of the timeliness of content and the nature of the approach, namely, event-specific content. However, there *is* a growing body of knowledge that is content streamed and/or delivered through web links to PowerPoint contents or texts that resulted from conference, summit, and association meetings. While some of this content was reviewed, the ephemeral nature of WebWeb (but unpublished) conference proceedings, for example, was not included.

Other content not included in the appendix but extensive in nature includes global emergency management, risk management, and disaster recovery information. In addition, content not available in the appendix due to a lack of research and publication or possibly due to content available but behind institutional firewalls includes unique aspects of disaster recovery or emergency management. It includes historic architecture; contemporary/more current resources and special needs of cultural institutions, such as museums; prevention and recovery from mischief and vandalism; more content on pestilence, insects, and infestations; and disaster planning and children.

Appendix B includes examples of forms, and Appendix C includes virtual world emergency simulations.

ARTICLES

As in most other areas of professional literature, hundreds of articles exist in popular and scholarly publications. Most articles, however, tend to contain either detailed coverage of a single event or specific ways to handle one narrow event or particular content related to an emergency or disaster. The articles included in this list represent both popular and scholarly publications, "lessons learned" through action or inaction taken, recommendations for action based on research and practice, and examples or templates to follow in similar or related situations. In addition, other than a number of unique or classic articles, those chosen for this list are dated post 9/11.

Anglim, Christopher. "The Worst Thing That Could Happen: Law Library Disasters and Preparing for the Unimaginable." *AALL Spectrum* 1, no. 4 (Dec. 1996): 8–19. Good general overview of a disaster-preparedness plan with content that includes fire, hazardous materials, computer emergencies, explosions, medical emergencies, natural disasters, power failures, shelving or structural collapse, and water damage or flooding.

Beinhoff, Lisa A. "Library Earthquake Preparedness Planning: How to Make Sure That Your Library Is Ready for the Big One." *Journal of Library Administration* 31, no. 1 (2000): 67–83. Good pre–9/11 guide with extensive information specific to earthquakes but includes earthquake-related issues, such as fire and water damage.

Bolger, Laurie. "Scared or Prepared? Disaster Planning Makes the Difference." *Information Outlook* 7, no. 7 (2003): 26–30. Designed to motivate individuals to plan for future disasters by emphasizing benefits.

Boss, Richard W. *Disaster Planning for Computers and Networks*. Chicago: Public Library Association, 2002, available at http://www.ala.org/ala/pla/plapubs/technotes/disasterplanning.cfm (accessed 9 June 2008). A technology disaster focus with recommended content on risk assessment and reduction covering prevention and recovery with common disaster plan elements for servers, the network, and clients as well as recovery recommendations covering communication, designated operators, designated managers, external resources, and insurance.

Cassell, Gracelyn. "Library Experiences with Natural Disasters: Hurricanes and Volcanoes (Montserrat)." *International Preservation News* 34 (2000): 4–11, available at http://www.ifla.org/VI/4/news/ipnn34.pdf (accessed 10 June 2008). Included as an entry in the Special Library Association Web portal on emergencies and focusing on recovery of materials and resources after a more frequently occurring natural disaster—a hurricane—and a more unusual disaster, disastrous effects from a volcano.

Clifton, Gerard. "Risk and Preservation Management of Digital Collections." *International Preservation News* 36 (Sept. 2005): 21–23, available at http://www.ifla.org/VI/4/news/ipnn36.pdf (accessed 10 June 2008). An unusual brief recovery discussion for digital materials with general but helpful recommendations.

DiMattia, Susan S. "A Gem of a Plan." *Information Outlook* 11, no. 6 (June 2007): 26–32. Relatively brief content but good breadth of coverage of fifty different emergencies and disasters with planning recommendations.

———. "Planning for Continuity." *Library Journal* (November 15, 2001): 32–34. The concept of business continuity is the focus of this post-9/11 article on how library and information centers coped with and attempted to recover from attacks.

Eng, Sidney. "How Technology and Planning Saved My Library at Ground Zero." *Computers in Library* 22, no. 4 (April 2002): 28–35, available at http://www.infotoday.com/cilmag/apr02/eng.htm (accessed 10 June 2008). Good preventive recommendations for how to design library technology to allow services to continue after disasters.

Hackbart-Dean, Pamela. "Shelter from the Storm: Disaster Prevention and Planning." *North Carolina Libraries*, 58, no. 3 (Fall 2000): 48–53. A focus on natural disasters and the roles libraries play for communities.

Hendrix, Lolita. "Will You Be Ready When Disaster Strikes?" *NonProfit World*, 18, no. 3, (May/June 2000): 32–36. A good basic approach for working with staff to ask the right questions for building emergency plans.

Higginbotham, Barbara Buckner. "Managing Emergencies: Small Construction Projects." *Technicalities* 1 (1996): 12–14. Good "lessons

learned" approach regarding a routine remodeling and expansion project that resulted in a pervasive concrete dust emergency.

Howes, Robert. "After the Disaster: Drawing Up the Insurance Claim."
ASLIB Proc. 5 (2003): 181–187. Much needed advice that stresses the
importance of keeping accurate records and statistics with practical information on—among other critical insurance issues—filing claims
after disasters.

Journal of the American Institute for Conservation 39 (Spring 2000): 1–
183. Excellent, extensive content in the entire issue devoted to preservation and conservator issues for library materials, resources, and
facilities.

Keiser, Barbie E. "Web as Safety Net: Weather-Related Catastrophes
and Other Natural Disasters." *Searcher* 10, no. 1 (Jan. 2002): 68–83.
A dated but classic look at the extensive growing world of technology
support for individuals and institutions prior to, during, and following
natural disasters and emergencies.

Lederer, Naomi, and Douglas J. Ernest. "Managing the Media During
a Library Crisis." *American Libraries* (Dec. 2003): 32–33. Specific to
Colorado State University but has valuable, detailed information and
recommendations to use in disaster plans regarding communication in
general and specifically "what should happen" in the controversial
arena of media misrepresentation.

Matthews, Graham. "Disaster Management: Sharing Experience, Working Together, Across the Sector." *Journal of Librarianship & Information Science* 37, no. 2 (June 2005): 63–74. Good content to add to
disaster plans with a focus on partnerships and collaborations before
and during disasters.

Muir, Adrienne, and Sarah Shenton. "If the Worst Happens: The Use
and Effectiveness of Disaster Plans in Libraries and Archives." *Library
Management* 23 (2002): 115–123. Noting the 2002 date, a good set of
recommendations on what works and doesn't work in print-based disaster plans with lessons for moving to contemporary formats, including the need to keep contact lists up-to-date, partnership and
collaborative failures, lack of planning for conservator processes, lack
of and inappropriate disaster supplies, and lack of attention to both
staff and constituent health and safety processes and directives.

Myles, Barbara. "The Impact of a Library Flood on Computer Operations." *Computers in Libraries* 20, no. 1 (Jan. 2000): 44–49. A basic,
although brief, source on primary and secondary issues (water and
other) during and post library flooding.

Schlotzhauer, Nonny. "Disaster Relief: Starting Points for Learning."
College & Research Libraries News 67, no. 2 (2006): 91–96, available
at http://www.ala.org/ala/acrl/acrlpubs/crlnews/backissues2006/febru
ary06/disasterrelief .cfm (accessed 9 June 2008). A good beginning
contemporary list for the bigger disaster relief picture that is designed
to provide content for academic libraries but is of value to other types
of institutions as well.

Silverman, Randy. "A Litany of Terrible, No Good, Very Bad Things Can
Happen After the Disaster." *International Preservation News* 33 (Sept.
2004): 8–15, available at http://www.ifla.org/VI/4/news/ipnn33.pdf (accessed 10 June 2008). A global but detailed checklist for assessment of
post-disaster recovery activities with a focus on materials and resources
recovery.

Stremple, Rosalie, and Michael F. Martone. "Disasters Come in All
Sizes." *Infopro* 2, no. 1 (March 2000): 29–35, available at http://www
.arma.org/pdf/articles/DisasterAllSizes.pdf (accessed 9 June 2008).
ARMA focus on data recovery with excellent exercise for testing emergency planning processes.

Swartz, Nikki. "Dealing with Disaster." *Information Management Journal* 40, no. 4 (2006): 28–34. A frequently cited author and article that
outlines the role of records managers and the issues related to the exclusion of these managers from post-disaster recovery environments
and the consequences of exclusion.

Todaro, Julie. "Managing Through Tragedy." *Library Administration &
Management*, 16, no. 1 (Winter 2002): 40–43. Written the week of 9/
11, this article focuses on the importance of managing the human aspects in response to disaster, emergency, and tragedy.

Villadsen, Alice W., and Gerardo E. de los Santos, eds. "Hoping for the
Best While Preparing for the Worst: Disasters, Emergencies, and the
Community College." Leadership Abstracts: *League Connections.*
League for Innovation in the Community College. HopingfortheBest
.pdf. 75p. 2007. Excellent content covering the roles and responsibili-

ties of community colleges in emergencies, including the murder of a student, tornadoes, hurricanes, and related disasters, such as floods and fires and the use of a community college as an emergency shelter.
Winston, Mark D., and Susan Quinn. "Library Leadership in Times of Crisis and Change." *New Library World* 106, no. 9/10 (2005): 395–415. A focus on research literature regarding libraries, crises, and change in the context of war, terrorism, and natural disasters, among a number of other societal issues.

MATERIALS FOR CHILDREN AND YOUTH

At first glance, including materials and resources for children and youth in this list seems unusual. However, when addressing constituents, library and information professionals often need to provide content and tailor messages for specific groups, including children and youth, parents, caregivers, educators of children and youth, and others who work with and for children and youth. There are many more resources for these constituents, including descriptions of disasters and emergencies, emergency vehicles, and emergency personnel. Many standard or classic resources, such as FEMA and Homeland Security, now have children or "kids" sections. In addition to content that informs children and youth about these issues, resources cited in this list include those that explain how to work with children and youth and examples of materials on how to explain emergency and disaster issues as well as expected critical behavior for the very youngest in this constituent group.

Children's Safety Zone, available at http://www.sosnet.com/safety/safety1.html. (accessed 8 May 2008). Diverse links to children's and youth safety resources in federal agencies and commercial websites.
Cleaver, Karen, and Janet Webb. *Emergency Care of Children and Young People*. Oxford, UK: Blackwell Publishing Ltd., 2007. A book designed

to provide extensive information for health professions, this content includes valuable information for those dealing with children and youth in other emergency settings, such as preparing those who work with children for emergency situations, legal and ethical practices, effective practices for communicating with children through distraction and play, minor injuries that might occur in the workplace, injury assessment and issues relating to drug and substance abuse, and self-harm.

Disaster Resources. Children, Stress, and Natural Disasters. University of Illinois Extension, available at http://www.ag.uiuc.edu/~disaster/teacher/teacher.html (accessed 1 May 2008). Good activities for teachers and parents.

Federal Emergency Management Administration. FEMA. Chicago: Heinemann Library, 2003, available at http://www.fema.gov (accessed 9 May 2008). FEMA resources (under "Websites") include extensive full-text content under fema.gov/kids (games, stories, K–12 curriculum) available for easy downloading with continuously updated information directed toward (along with profit and nonprofit business environments) families, youth and children in work, and school and home settings as well as during travel and fun/vacation settings.

Gibbons, Gail. *Emergency!* New York: Holiday House, 1994. Gibbons, one of the most successful juvenile nonfiction authors, offers an informative but nonthreatening picture book for ages three and above with a visual trip through emergency vehicles, first responders, and emergency situations and solutions to problems in these settings as well as a range of emergencies and disasters to experience.

Graham, Ian. *Emergency!* Laguna Hills, CA: QED Publishing, 2006. Extensive, detailed color and black and white, photographic look at emergency vehicles as well as unique machines and unique uses for vehicles and machines with a focus on rescue on land, water, and in the air for young children.

Helping Children Cope with Disaster. Federal Citizen Information Center Home Page, available at http://www.pueblo.gsa.gov/cic_text/family/children-disaster/children.htm (accessed 8 May 2008). Excellent developmentally appropriate content delivered by age with recommendations for assisting children in coping with emergencies and disasters.

Kalman, Bobbie. *Emergency Workers Are on Their Way!* St. Catharines, ON Canada: Crabtree Pub., 2005. For older children ages seven to twelve, Kalman offers emergency rescue information in an exciting, yet reassuring way with a variety of types of workers, both men and women in this series title, from a variety of organizations and representing diverse cultures and ethnicities. It focuses on different types of emergencies, including wildlife rescues and water rescues in both urban and rural locations.

Kids.gov. Federal Citizen Information Center Home Page, available at http://www.kids.gov (accessed 8 May 2008). Children's and youth searchable gateway to all U.S. government resources, including content designed for Kids.gov.

Levine, Peter A., and Maggie Kline. *Trauma-Proofing Your Kids: A Parents' Guide for Instilling Joy, Confidence and Resilience.* Berkeley, CA: North Atlantic Books, 2008. A much-needed-don't-miss title that helps parents, grandparents, and other relatives as well as teachers and caregivers in both prevention and treatment of trauma in kids for specific situations as well as twenty-first century life for children. Extraordinary resource.

Lu, Mei-Yu. "Children's Literature in a Time of Tragedy." ERIC Digest, 2001, available at http://www.ericdigests.org/2002–2/time.htm (accessed 2 April 2008). Specific suggestions for helping children as well as annotated citations of content to assist in the process.

Masoff, Joy. *Emergency!* New York: Scholastic, 1999. A focus for seven- to twelve-year-olds on emergency medical personnel (responding to accidents and illness), their vehicles, and their tools and equipment (typical and unusual) in both health care and first-responder careers for patients and families of patients.

Mayo, Margaret. *Emergency!* Minneapolis, MN: Carolrhoda Books, 2002. Rescue vehicles for diverse emergencies, including sinking boats, traffic and transportation disasters, fires, floods, snowstorms and blizzards, and lost individuals, with reassuring rescue messages.

National Fire Protection Association, available at http://www.nfpa.org/ (accessed 6 June 2008). Extensive web content with children's and youth materials throughout the site as well as specific to the Sparky, the Fire Dog campaign.

Orndorff, John C., and Suzanne Harper. *Access Board Resources on Emergency Evacuation and Disaster Preparedness.* New York: Abrams Books for Young Readers, 2007. Detailed sets of scenarios to prepare young people/young adults to deal with emergencies, including big picture events such as surviving terrorist attacks and surviving weather disasters to more narrowly focused events like safe Internet behavior and recommended first-aid kits.

Raatma, Lucia. *Safety During Emergencies.* Chanhassen, MN: Childs World, 2003. A "Living Well" series monograph that provides good information on natural disasters and more "typical" weather disasters as well as (unfortunately) more contemporary emergencies, such as acts of violence, with a glossary.

Thompson, Tamara. *Emergency Response.* Farmington Hills, MI: Lucent Books, 2004. A career series title for young adults (seventh grade and up as well as career counselors) with emergency responder information on fire fighters, law enforcement, and medical personnel that includes career issues, such as gender, salaries, training, and advancement as well as competencies needed.

MISCELLANEOUS

This section—typically used for content not covered in other subject categories—includes unusual formats (as well as links recommending video content), a few conference proceedings, and a few unique approaches to the general subject of emergency management.

Back in Business: Disaster Recovery/Business Resumption, DVD. Commonwealth Films, Inc.; *The Best Defense: A User's Guide to Computer Security Today*, DVD. Commonwealth Films, Inc.; *Computer Virus Attack: Defending Against Viruses and Hackers*, DVD. Commonwealth Films, Inc.; and *Ready for Anything: Business Continuity, Disaster Recovery, Preparedness*, DVD. Commonwealth Films, Inc. An often-cited series of no-nonsense recommendations for prevention and recovery of technology for rapid return to business continuity.

Emergency Response and Salvage Wheel, realia. National Institute for the Conservation of Cultural Property in cooperation with the National Task Force on Emergency Response: Washington, DC: The Institute, 1997, available at http://www.heritagepreservation.org/PROGRAMS/Wheel1.htm. A unique, don't miss, detailed tool for determining recovery treatment and handling for cultural resources.

Metaversed. *Emergency Training in Second Life,* available at http://meta versed.com/23–jul–2007/emergency-training-second-life (accessed 22 June 2008). Fascinating website providing information on unique responder training in a newer simulation environment, Second Life.

National Fire Protection Association, available at http://www.nfpa.org. (accessed 9 May 2008). Extensive content (Learn Not to Burn) directed to children and youth and provided by age/grade level including: K–3 curriculum, coloring books, educational videos, babysitting materials, procedures for reporting fires, and evacuating for children and youth.

Videos on Preservation. Preservation, University of California, San Diego: Education and Awareness for Library Users, available at http://gort.ucsd.edu/preseduc/video.htm (accessed 10 April 2008). Ten plus videos, both classic and contemporary, on more of the "big picture" preservation issues as well as the narrower print/book dust and "general care" instructions and issues, for example.

MONOGRAPHS

Hundreds of popular and scholarly monographs exist on emergency management and disaster recovery. The monographs in this list include both popular and scholarly material; however, as with articles, other than unique or classic information, publication dates are post-9/11 due to the sheer volume of content.

Abkowitz, Mark D. *Operational Risk Management: A Case Study Approach to Effective Planning and Response.* Hoboken, NJ: John Wiley & Sons, Inc., 2008. Case studies (9/11, Bhopal, and Hyatt Walkway Collapse) show a close look at prevention, management, and recovery of disasters and emergencies. This includes natural, man-made, and political acts, such as terrorist acts, with recommendations for strategic planning focusing on lessons learned and future prevention.

Adams, Cheryl. *Hostile Planet: The Essential Guide to Surviving Natural Disasters, Pandemic, and Terrorist Attacks.* Bloomington, IN: Author-House, 2006. A self-published monograph with good reviews that is described as a virtual encyclopedia of disasters and emergencies and "how to survive them" recommendations, including more "typical" weather disasters as well as the atypical, such as heat, tsunamis, landslides, radiation exposure, bird flu, viruses, plagues, fevers, and poisons.

Alire, Camila, ed. *Library Disaster Planning and Recovery Handbook.* Edison, NJ: Neal-Schuman Publishers, 2000. A classic, always-recommended guide with extensive recommendations by authors who have lived through a flood and all related disasters and survived.

Arnold, Christopher, Jack Lyons, James Munger, Rebecca C. Quinn, and Thomas L Smith. *Guide for Improving Safety in Earthquakes, Floods, and High Winds. Risk Management Series. FEMA 424.* Washington, DC: Federal Emergency Management Agency (FEMA), 2004. A unique school building and school population target audience for this detailed manual for handling natural disasters, such as earthquakes, floods, and winds.

Arnot, Bob, and Mark Cohen. *Your Survival: The Complete Resource for Disaster and Planning and Recovery.* Long Island City, NY: Hatherleigh Press, Ltd,, 2007. A monograph and DVD for families but very applicable to businesses and institutions concerning natural disasters with checklists, assessments, and access to a survival website with nonfiction narrative of lessons learned.

Ballofett, Nelly, and Jenny Hille. *Preservation and Conservation for Libraries and Archives.* Chicago: American Library Association, 2004. Good basic content on preservation and conservation for prevention as well as treatment, including setting up work spaces and recommended supplies and techniques for prevention as well as recovery.

Black, Dave. *What to Do When the Shit Hits the Fan.* New York: Skyhorse Publishing Company, Inc., 2007. Now that the title has the reader's attention, readers receive detailed assistance for all businesses, environments, and individuals in the areas of communication and med-

ical needs, including basic survival issues related to food, water, and
shelter.

Buck, George. *Foundations of Emergency Management.* Florence, KY:
Thomas Delmar Learning, 2009. With reviews of the only available
content in May of 2008, this monograph promises to be a comprehensive management tool for working in partnerships across local, state,
and national jurisdictions as well as for defining the role of a high-tech
emergency manager.

Bullock, Jane A. *Introduction to Homeland Security.* Amsterdam, The
Netherlands: Butterworth-Heinemann, Elsevier, 2006. Extensive content with history, statutory authority, definitions and rationale, best
practices, and sample plans.

Bumgarner, Jeffrey B. *Emergency Management: A Reference Handbook.*
Santa Barbara, CA: ABC-CLIO, Inc., 2008. Considered an extensive
non-technical guide to all aspects of emergency management including
natural and manmade disasters; lists and timelines; history, policies,
and procedures.

California Governor's Office, Los Angeles. Office of Emergency Services:
*Earthquake Preparedness 101: Guidelines for Colleges and Universi-
ties.* 2000. Emergency management and business continuity higher education guidelines for earthquake areas with sample job descriptions
for emergency personnel, legislative content, sample disaster plans, a
planning checklist for campus building evacuation, and information on
state and federal assistance.

Canton, Lucien G. *Emergency Management: Concepts and Strategies for
Effective Programs.* Hoboken, NJ: John Wiley & Sons, Inc., 2006.
Practical content, including the role of emergency personnel, designing an emergency management program, and crisis management with
case studies.

Casavant, David A. *Emergency Preparedness for Facilities: A Guide to
Safety Planning and Business Continuity.* Rockville, MD: Government
Institutes, ABS Consulting, 2003. Excellent resource with detailed ex-
planations of natural and nonnatural events, steps in and examples of
strategic planning, best practices in designing the disaster plan, training for emergencies and disasters, recovery, mitigation guidelines, and
eighty-plus pages of appendices with a CD with forms for customization.

Cauthern, Cynthia. *Red Alert: Becoming Self-Sufficient for the Next Bioterrorist Attack and Flu Pandemic.* Bloomington, IN: iUniverse, Inc., 2006. Detailed approach to achieving self-sufficiency during a terrorist attack or a pandemic occurrence including evacuation, and likely threats.

Childs, Donna R. *Prepare for the Worst, Plan for the Best: Disaster Preparedness and Recovery for Small Businesses.* Hoboken, NJ: John Wiley & Sons, Inc., 2008. Emergency management and disaster recovery guide for businesses including prevention and recovery regarding technology (hardwired and wireless,) data and infrastructure, power issues, communication, web-based information with sample plans.

Dorge, Valerie, and Sharon L. Jones, eds. *Building an Emergency Plan: A Guide for Museums and Other Cultural Institutions.* Los Angeles: The Getty Conservation Institute, 1999. Older, solid content that focuses on the unique aspects (resources, facilities, etc.) of preventing and "saving" cultural resources.

Earthquake Preparedness Checklist for Schools. Los Angeles: Southern California Earthquake Preparedness Project (SCEPP), 1999. K–12 guide to earthquakes emergency management, including basic destruction prevention, evacuation, structural and nonstructural hazards, critical communication processes, and records protection.

Edwards Disaster Recovery Directory. Combo Book + CD: 2007 Edition Hardcopy + CD. Ashton, MD: Edwards Information, LLC, 2007. Considered the most extensive resource for thousands of vendor listings with over four hundred categories.

Fire, Frank L. *Common Sense Dictionary for First Responders.* Tulsa, OK: Fire Engineering Books & Videos, 2006. A glossary of terms useful to responders in emergency situations as well as to individuals in institutions finding themselves managing a crisis, including content on hazardous materials, environmental issues, emergency medical services (EMS), and hazmat clothing, with a glossary to assist in designing emergency/disaster plans and training materials.

Fortson, Judith. *Disaster Planning and Recovery: A How to Do It Manual for Librarians and Archivists.* New York: Neal-Schuman Publishers, 1992. An older, but well-received guide for emergency prevention, preparedness, response, and recovery.

Genovese, Robert. *Disaster Preparedness Manual*. New York: William S. Hein & Co, 2003, at http://www.law.arizona.edu/library/disastermanual.com. Current, extensive manual for a law library but applicable to all types of libraries.

Gottschalk, Jack. *Crisis Management*. Oxford: Capstone Publishing Ltd., 2002. Crisis management with cases, scenario, and examples for businesses, including an extensive glossary.

Grabel, Joyce Ann, and Elaine Stattler. *Employer's Guide to Disaster Readiness and Recovery*. New York: Aspen Publishers, 2007. A significant source (presented in a three-ring binder for flexibility and directed to employers) with general content, extensive checklists, employee safety guidelines, customer relations, business continuity, and compliance.

Gustin, Joseph F. *Disaster and Recovery Planning: A Guide for Facility Managers*. Lilburn, GA: Fairmont Press, Inc., 2007. With a business continuity focus: disaster planning regulatory influences, fire safety, bomb threats, earthquakes, computer and data protection, power systems, and crisis planning.

Haddow, George D., Jane A. Bullock, and Damon P. Coppola. *Introduction to Emergency Management*. Burlington, MA: Elsevier, 2007. Comprehensive text on the disaster management and other emergencies with current practices, roles, and responsibilities that focus on avoiding—during disasters—breakdowns in communication and leadership and case methods using real, well-known examples.

Halstead, Deborah, Richard Jasper, and Felicia Little. *Disaster Planning: A How-to-Do-It Manual with Planning Templates on CD-ROM*. New York: Neal-Schuman, 2005. Still current, well-reviewed manual with software to allow for customization of checklists, procedures, and policy design.

Harmon, J. *Integrated Pest Management in Museum, Library, and Archival Facilities: A Step by Step Approach for the Design, Development, Implementation, and Maintenance of an Integrated Pest Management Program*. Indianapolis, IN: 1993. Available from Harmon Preservation Pest Management, P.O. Box 40262, Indianapolis, IN, 46240. Basic manual—somewhat dated but useable—for monitoring, identification, and treatments (nonchemical and chemical) for pest control of pests and insects.

Harrison, Kathy. *Just in Case.* North Adams, MA: Storey Publishing, LLC, 2008. Although this is a "recovery" focus written primarily for home environments, there is valuable information for any/all environments where natural and/or man-made disasters and emergencies might result in prolonged power outages sheltering in place and/or evacuation with nutrition, heating, cooling, and personal supply issues that have especially valuable content for communication plans when individuals are separated.

Henry, Julie. *Home Emergency Packet Guide: Clear, Concise and Practical, Before–During–After Guidelines.* Tigard, OR: Informed Publishing, 2007. Prevention and recovery focus on preparedness from careful selection and appropriate placement of supplies to plans for assessment of use/need for additional materials.

Hill, Peregrine, Sarah Ellington, Edward Bishop, Sarah Hamilton, John Morrell, and Paul Stagg. *Emergency Services: Law and Liability.* Bristol, UK: Jordans Publishing Ltd., 2006. Not typical library content but valuable information for managers writing disaster plans and training staff on law and liability regarding what they can and can't do for constituents, families of constituents, and employees and volunteers.

Hill, Tara. *Helpful Hints for School Emergency Management: Emergency "Go-Kits."* Washington, DC: Emergency Response and Crisis Management (ERCM) Technical Assistance (TA) Center, 2006. A K–12 focus with excellent information on policies and protocols; emergency supply kits or "go-kits"; communication needs including staff and student identification and descriptions; first aid, medical issues, and dietary needs; and reunification plans for students and family members.

Howitt, Arnold M., and Herman B. Leonard, eds. *Managing Crises: Responses to Large-Scale Emergencies.* Washington, DC: CQ Press, 2008. Larger-scale emergencies aren't typically the purview of library managers, but case methods provide excellent content for organization of information and design of disaster plans for libraries as well as roles of responsibilities managers might have within larger, umbrella organizations.

Kahn, Miriam. *Disaster Response and Planning for Libraries.* 2nd ed. Chicago: American Library Association, 2003. Considered an expert in the field, Kahn offers an updated manual (from her two titles in the

1990s) on designing a plan as well as significant appendices of forms and templates.

————. *The Library Security and Safety Guide to Prevention, Planning, and Response*. Chicago: American Library Association, 2008. Expert Kahn expands her disaster management and emergency expertise by focusing on security, including possible problems and strategies for success.

————. *Protecting Your Library's Digital Sources: The Essential Guide to Planning and Preservation*. Chicago: ALA Editions of the American Library Association, 2004. Rather than big-picture prevention and planning, the focus is on plans returning resources to acceptable levels for business continuity as well as materials and resources recovery, including the more typical print materials and more unique materials, such as sculpture (three-dimensional), paintings, photographs, and audiovisuals.

Lahidji, Reza, and Stephanie Poston. *Disaster Information Needs of Ethnic Minorities in the U.S.* Darby, PA: DIANE Publishing Company, 2007. A unique, exemplary guide for "translating" emergency management and disaster planning information for special populations who may have special needs, including focused self-assessment content and potential hazard assessment and recovery.

Lewis, Bernard T., and Richard P. Payant. *The Facility Manager's Emergency Preparedness Handbook*. New York: AMACOM Books, 2003. Solid, helpful content for library managers with responsibility for facilities, including prevention and preparedness organization regarding materials and resources placement, labeling, and training.

Lundin, Cody. *When all Hell Breaks Loose: Stuff You Need to Survive When Disaster Strikes*. Layton, UT: Gibbs Smith, Publisher, 2007. Survival focus for home, work, and public environments with valuable information for managers or employees, including the more typical supplies needed and used as well as mental and emotional issues and ways to avoid panic with no-nonsense language.

Matthews, Graham, and John Feather. *Disaster Management for Libraries and Archives*. Aldershot, Hampshire UK: Ashgate Publishing, 2003. Solid coverage of general library resource planning and recovery with more information on archival content than other library disaster plan monographs.

Minnesota Department of Education. *Emergency Planning and Procedures Guide for Schools*. Minneapolis: Minnesota Department of Public Safety Division of Homeland Security and Emergency Management, 2005. General guidelines and updated content on critical procedures and policies designed to be customized per each campus/school building, specific district policy, and local community disaster plans with tagged pages for assistance in designing training materials.

Mirolla, Michael. *Always Read: A to Z Guide to Disaster Preparedness*. Indianapolis, IN: Sam Technical Publishing, LLC, 2008. A focus on prevention through extensive preparedness on securing home but applicable to work environments as well for all types of disasters with unique and extensive information on technology disasters as well.

Pine, John C. *Emergency Management Technology*. Hoboken, NJ: John Wiley & Sons, Inc., 2006. In-depth look at technology in support of emergency management and disaster recovery including the Internet, networks, radio, cable, telephones, messaging systems, and warning systems with a focus on software systems designed specifically for emergency processes.

Pinkowski, Jack. *Disaster Management Handbook*. Boca Raton, FL: CRC Press, Taylor & Francis Group, 2008. A nontechnical complete guide to emergency management as a profession with cases that offer first-person accounts and analyses of emergencies ranging from airplane crashes to computer network hacking and covering working with individual agencies as well as attempting to coordinate local, state, and federal agencies and activities.

Project Impact: Building a Disaster Resistant Community. Washington, DC: Federal Emergency Management Agency (FEMA), 1997. Older but recommended FEMA title due to a unique look at the leadership, partnerships, collaborations, assessments, and planning needed to design a best practice community-based emergency management plan with forms and checklists.

Rothstein, Philip Jan, ed. *Disaster Recovery Testing: Exercising Your Contingency Plan*. Brookfield, CT: Rothstein Associates, Inc., 2007. Very unique, expertly vetted (thirty professionals) diverse contingency plans.

Stilwell, Alexander. *The Encyclopedia of Survival Techniques, New and Revised.* Guilford, CT: Globe Pequot Press, 2008. Timely, complete, and unusual best-selling title with unusual disasters and "how to survive" self-defense techniques illustrated with extensive drawings to assist in surviving, among dozens of other natural and man-made disasters, car jacking, road-rage incidents, terrorists, and suspicious situations, such as packages or an individual's behavior.

Thenell, Jan. *Library's Crisis Communications Planner: A PR Guide for Handling Every Emergency.* Chicago: American Library Association, 2004. Good, solid guide for successful media relations before, during, and after disasters and emergencies.

U.S. Department of Education. *Emergency Evacuation of People with Physical Disabilities from Buildings: 2004 Conference Proceedings (Rockville, Maryland, October 13–14, 2004).* Washington, DC: Emergency Response and Crisis Management (ERCM) Technical Assistance (TA) Center, 2005. Critical element of emergency management typically skimmed over or little known by managers with a focus on individual situations, techniques, and equipment to aid in successful evacuation for special populations.

Werner, Daniel J. *Emergency Response: Before, During and After.* Gambier, OH: Xoxoxo Press, 2006. A guide book with CD-ROM for the design and customization of emergency action plans in higher education for managers with security roles and responsibilities.

WEBSITES

Thousands of websites exist for emergency management, disaster recovery, and related areas. Standard information literacy assessment of websites was employed to sort out content based on "author" credentials, credibility of supporting or umbrella organizations, and (if appropriate) currency citation analysis. The websites included here represent .gov, .org, .net, .edu, and some .com content and because of the dynamic nature and enormous number of possibilities of first tier, second tier, and third tier content and web pages as well as related links, website annotations will illustrate any unique or not-to-be missed content. In addition, if a website was included primarily because of its use as an example or template, the words "example/template" will be included in the annotation. Readers should note that the dates indicated as access dates for websites should all be for the month of June 2008, given that the fact check review to determine the correct web address occurred in June 2008. In reality, sites were accessed repeatedly throughout the fall of 2007 and the spring of 2008.

Advice for Safeguarding Buildings against Chemical or Biological Attack.
Indoor Environment Department at Lawrence Berkeley National Laboratory, available at http://securebuildings.lbl.gov/ (accessed 23 June 2008). Atypical disasters (chemical, biological, and radiological attacks) with recommendations for public buildings with prevention, management, and recovery information.

American Institute for Conservation of Historic and Artistic Works.
Washington, DC: AIC, n.d., available at http://aic.stanford.edu/ (accessed 9 May 2008). Primarily a conservator expert online environment with recommendations, under "Public Info" on conservation guides for unique materials and personal "treasures."

American Medical Association. American Medical Association (AMA), available at http://www.ama-assn.org/ama/pub/category/6206.html (accessed 24 June 2008). Over five hundred resources available from the AMA including resources from the *Center for Public Health Preparedness and Disaster Response* (CPHPDR, a major educational resource) and bioterrorism information including anthrax, viruses, bacteria, and toxins for individuals, families, managers, and employees in both military and civilian life.

American Red Cross. American Red Cross, available at http://www
.redcross.org (accessed 25 June 2008). Extensive Red Cross resources linked from the home website, including children's materials, *Get Prepared* (preparedness and prevention), available at http://www.redcross
.org/services/prepare/0,1082,0_239_,00.html (accessed 25 June 2008); unique critical information *Disaster Preparedness for Persons with Disabilities*, available at http://www.redcross.org/services/disaster/be-prepared/disability.pdf (accessed 24 June 2008); basic disaster services

provided by Red Cross, *Disaster Services*, available at http://www
.redcross.org/services/disaster/ (accessed 16 June 2008); and seasonal
emergency content.

California Preservation Program. Washington, DC: Institute for Museum and Library Services, available at http://calpreservation.org/info/
index.html (accessed 5 May 2008). Excellent disaster recovery content
including significant content for recovery on-site (libraries, archives,
historical societies, records repositories, and cultural institutions) and
consulting services, online information resources, and education on
preservation techniques and preservation management as well as collections maintenance and excellent samples. These include "Generic
Disaster Plan Workbook," a "Library Disaster Plan" template, sample
exercises and sample plans, hazards surveys, and curriculum on library
disaster planning from Island Empire Libraries Disaster Response
Network.

CBS News Disaster Links. Columbia Broadcasting System, available at
http://www.cbsnews.com/digitaldan/disaster/disasters.shtml (accessed
23 June 2008). Hundreds of links to news and news-related sites with
extensive content on disaster events and recovery, preparedness, prevention, management, and recovery.

Contingency Planning & Management. Contingency Planning & Management, availble at http://www.contingencyplanning.com (accessed
23 June 2008). Provides links to resources on-site as well as links to
recommended sample guides, manuals, templates, news stories, and
articles.

Department of Elder Affairs. Florida, available at http://elder
affairs.state.fl.us/ (accessed 8 May 2008). Provides excellent don't-miss
information on unique emergency management and recovery needs of
older Americans.

Department of Homeland Security. Department of Homeland Security,
available at www.dhs.gov (accessed 18 June 2008). Extensive content,
including much-cited resources on all types of disasters such as *Emergency Preparedness Tips* and first responder focus from the *FirstRes-
ponder.gov* portal to all federal government resources.

Disabled People and Disaster Planning. Disabled People and Disaster
Planning, available at http://www.citycent.com/dp2/index.html (ac-

cessed 25 June 2008). Older classic document with recommendations on unique needs of special populations during disasters and emergencies specifically for earthquakes and California, but actually applicable for all types and sizes of libraries in all types of natural and man-made situations.

Disaster & Emergency Plan. University of Florida, George A. Smathers Libraries, available at http://Web.uflib.ufl.edu/committees/disaster/in dex.html (accessed 20 June 2008). Always an excellent website for online best practices with emergency management coordinators shelter information; plans, policies, and procedures; and communication lists and content, such as contact people and signage.

Disaster Center. National Disaster Education Coalition. 1999, available at http://www.disastercenter.com/guide/resources.html. (accessed 9 May 2008). Excellent content and links to content on all types of natural disasters and information on "how to deal with disasters."

Disaster Committee. University of Kansas Libraries, available at http:// www.lib.ku.edu/preservation/Disaster.shtml (accessed 25 June 2008). Disaster Committee in Kansas with links to the state of Kansas disaster planning.

A Disaster Plan for Libraries and Archives. AMIGOS, available at http://www.amigos.org/files/disasterplan.pdf (accessed 25 June 2008). Bibliographic network sample disaster plan, links to best practice plans, and bibliography of emergency and disaster resources.

Disaster Plan Workbook. New York University, New York, available at http://www.nyu.edu/library/bobst/research/preserv/displan/ch1.htm (accessed 7 May 2008). Complete disaster plan workbook that allows the user to build a plan unique to their library.

Disaster Planning Portal. Special Libraries Association (SLA), available at http://www.sla.org/content/resources/inforesour/sept11help/disip/in dex.cfm (accessed 18 June 2008). Unique association portal updated post-9/11 and dedicated to librarians lost in the tower attacks with print and online resources linked.

Disaster Preparation and Recovery. Medline Plus, available at http://www .nlm.nih.gov/medlineplus/disasterpreparationandrecovery.html (accessed 20 June 2008). Excellent website with consistently quality resources on medical, health, first aid information, and recommendations.

Disaster Preparedness. Disaster Mitigation Planning Assistance, available at http://matrix.msu.edu/~disaster/index.php (accessed 16 June 2008). Don't-miss best practices examples loaded and maintained in a searchable database with content from all types and sizes of libraries and archives.

Disaster Preparedness and Recovery. Chicago: American Library Association, 2007, available at http://www.ala.org/ala/washoff/woissues/disasterpreparedness/distrprep.cfm (accessed 8 May 2008). A number of good resources recommended as well as online links, including collection valuation and preservation of materials and resources.

Disaster Preparedness and Response. Conservation OnLine Document Library, available at http://palimpsest.stanford.edu/bytopic/disasters/ (accessed 16 June 2008). Constantly cited and linked to Conservation Online website with templates, forms, articles, and curriculum for collection maintenance and recovery.

Disaster Preparedness and Response for Schools and Universities. National Clearinghouse for Educational Facilities (NCEF), available at http://www.edfacilities.org/rl/disaster.cfm (accessed 23 June 2008). Higher education content designed primarily for disaster and emergency management of facilities with over eighty content links of additional related issues, events, and activities.

Disaster Preparedness Plan for Small Public Libraries—2002. State Library of Ohio, available at http://winslo.state.oh.us/services/LPD/disaster_frnt.html (accessed 25 June 2008). Much-cited links list of library disaster plans from much smaller library environments.

Disaster Prevention & Emergency Planning. MBK Consulting, available at http://www.mbkcons.com/wkshp/disaster/disasterfront.htm (accessed 16 June 2008). Commercial consultant/vendor site that includes free curriculum.

Disaster Psychiatry. American Psychiatry Association, available at http://www.psych.org/Resources/DisasterPsychiatry.aspx (accessed 8 May 2008). Excellent online resources, including the full text of the *Disaster Psychiatry Handbook; APA Disaster Psychiatry Materials* brochures on "anxiety and high alerts"; mental health resources recommended for use during natural disasters; and "how to talk to children" during disasters and emergencies.

Disaster Recovery Journal, available at http://www.drj.com/ (accessed 18 June 2008). An exemplary journal for all businesses and institutions but applicable to all types of libraries and levels of librarians and library staff: devoted to business continuity (appropriate for profit and non- or not-for-profit) with links to sample plans and outlines; best practices; web-based recovery plans; and an extensive not-to-be-missed glossary page at http://www.drj.com/glossary/glossary.htm.

Disaster Recovery Newsletter. TechRepublic, available at http://search .techrepublic.com.com/search/Disaster + Recovery + Newsletter.htm l?tag = nl.e061 (accessed 25 June 2008). Excellent online newsletter with free subscriptions and RSS feeds.

Disaster Recovery Planning. EDUCAUSE, available at http://connect .educause.edu/browse/content/node/237/list/feed (accessed 23 June 2008). Some content on-site as well as links to higher education websites and ongoing content regarding workshops.

Disaster Resource Guide, available at http://www.disaster-resource.com/ (accessed 16 June 2008). Solid resource including articles (twelve years of full text and citations), monographs, and websites including hundreds of vendors and resource websites.

Disaster Resources. Extension Services, University of Illinois; College of Agriculture, University of Illinois, available at http://www.ag.ui uc.edu/~disaster/facts/emotion.html (accessed15 May 2008). Unique disaster recovery content with excellent training curriculum on a variety of issues, including the emotional reactions and responses to a disaster (assisting with post-disaster stress issues).

Disaster Response and Recovery. National Archives, available at http://www.archives.gov/preservation/disaster-response/ (accessed 16 June 2008). A focus on conservation and preservation with some curriculum and training content.

DPlan: The Online Disaster-Planning Tool. Dplan, available at http://www.dplan.org/ (accessed 25 June 2008). A don't-miss free web-based template for designing disaster plans, password-protected remote storage of plans, generic update reminders for all sizes of institutions with realistic resources for medium-sized to the very smallest environment.

DRI International. DRI International, available at http://www.drii.org/

DRII/ (accessed 23 June 2008). Focus on business continuity plans but applicable to libraries/nonprofits.

Emergency Management Collection. New Jersey State Library, available at http://www.njstatelib.org/Research_Guides/Emergency_Manage ment/index.php (accessed 20 June 2008). Extensive guides to primarily print information for library managers and employees.

Environmental Protection Agency. U.S. Environmental Protection Agency, available at http://www.epa.gov. (accessed 10 May 2008). Excellent federal online resource with an "Emergencies" page that has dozens of links and training links; toxic materials assessment and management; and the EPA's "list of lists" on chemicals and emergency management, available at www.epa.gov/ceppo/pubs/title3.pdf.

Extension Disaster Education Network (EDEN). Extension Disaster Education Network (EDEN), available at http://eden.lsu.edu/ (accessed 23 June 2008). Online education resources, including education and research projects, speculation, and prediction on future disaster issues, and a communication plan.

Federal Emergency Management Agency (FEMA), available at http://www.fema.gov/ (accessed 16 June 2008). FEMA serves as the premier content area for emergency management and disaster recovery with many additional web environments (for example, ready.gov); a database of ancillary publications, including DVDs, monographs, audio/video clips, and so forth; best practices; samples; and both general and unique information for types of natural and man-made disasters. These include disaster plans; guides for businesses of all sizes; safety information for high-rise buildings as well as readiness and prevention kits and checklists for all types of buildings; awareness information and safety tips for all weather situations; assistance information for recovery for individuals and businesses; guidebooks and manuals; unique information for higher education, older Americans, individuals with disabilities; short-term and long-term data on recovery and salvage for diverse formats (*Interactive Emergency Response and Salvage Wheel*); extensive training content through the *Emergency Management Institute*; maps and time lines; specific content on disasters, such as fire; and extensive supply information for all situations and environments.

Free Management Library.org, available at http://www.freemanage
mentlibrary.org/ (accessed 25 June 2008). Easy-to-access, comprehensive resources regarding the leadership and management of an individual, other individuals, groups, and organizations.

Harvard University Libraries. Library Preservation, available at http://
preserve.harvard.edu/emergencies/index.html (accessed 5 May 2008).
Always cited content from Harvard includes *Library Collections Emergency Handbook*, policies and procedures, general resources needed,
and how to use them; vision and principles for managing library and
archival collections; and disaster and emergency recovery and tips on
care of personal or home collections of materials. http://preserve.har
vard.edu/guidelines/reformattingprinciples.html.

Health & Human Services/Office of Emergency Preparedness. U.S. Department of Health and Human Services, available at www.oep
.dhhs.gov/ (accessed 3 April 2008). Emergency management content
with a focus on health, medical, and recovery from major emergencies,
such as natural disasters, technological disasters, major transportation
accidents, and terrorism.

*Heritage Preservation: the National Institute for Conservation Field
Guide to Emergency Response.* Heritage Preservation, available at
www.heritagepreservation.org/ (accessed 2 May 2008). The National
Institute for Conservation is a preservation "wheel" that serves as a
tool to assist in planning and decision-making for cultural institutions.
The Heritage Preservation website offers additional information (often
unique to recent disaster issues, such as flooding content) and links
visitors to the *Heritage Emergency National Task Force on Emergency
Response* that offers highly recommended curriculum resources for
decision-making and training with techniques and recommendations
in *Tips for Salvaging Water Damaged Valuables*.

Higher Ed Crisis/Emergency Management Plan. Society of College and
University Planning (SCUP), available at http://www.scup.com (accessed 23 June 2008). Well respected, consistently cited, higher education extensive online content for administrators, including *Crises and
Disaster Management Planning for Higher Education* http://www
.scup.org/resources/topic_issue/crisis-disaster-mgmt.html that offers
full text resources, crises communication information (content and ex-

tensive links to higher education plans), and related upcoming SCUP events.

Homeland Security. U.S. Department of Homeland Security, available at http://www.dhs.org (accessed 3 March 2008). Discusses FEMA, the premier disaster recovery and emergency management federal agency with content, including extensive training curriculum (prevention and protection, travel security, and preparedness) for families. Also discusses nonprofit and profit business environments as well as links to ancillary programs, such as Citizen Corps (USA Freedom Corps), an organization created to coordinate local community volunteer activities to aid in any disaster and/or emergency situations.

Homeland Security Watch. BLOG. Managed by Jonah Czerwinski, 2005, available at http://www.hlswatch.com/ (accessed 11 April 2008). This is a news and commentary blog on homeland security issues with focus on preparedness, response, and infrastructure as well as border security for policy wonks. Has excellent up-to-date information for managers, especially those in local and statewide emergency-management community partnerships for preparedness and prevention.

Information Portals. SLA, available at http://www.sla.org/content/resources/infoportals/index.cfm (accessed 16 June 2008). SLA members-only web content with additional free online resources delivered to any user/nonmember and searchable using "disaster recovery."

International Association of Emergency Managers (IAEM). International Association of Emergency Managers (IEAM), available at http://www.iaem.com/ (accessed 18 June 2008). Although an association web environment, good resources for emergency managers, including training content, excellent recommendations on the communication message, and—specifically—a don't-miss emergency-manager principles document.

Internet Library for Librarians, available at http://www.itcompany.com/inforetriever.com (accessed 8 June 2008). A solid, general searchable portal for the profession of library and information science, with extensive link results through searching "emergency management."

The Internet Public Library, available at http://www.ipl.org/ (accessed 18 June 2008). Significant resources on emergency management and disaster preparedness and recovery with links to global resources like FEMA and extensive annotations.

LibraryLaw.com. LibraryLaw.com, available at http://www.librarylaw
.com/ (accessed 20 June 2008). Always recommended web environment with extensive state-by-state and federal links to critical content
regarding libraries and the law, including shelter legislation.

Library of Congress, available at http://lcWeb.loc.gov/ (accessed 5 May
2008). Extensive, well-respected classic and current content on emergency preparedness and disaster recovery, including content and recommendations on library security, procedures for care, and recovery
of both library and personal collections of diverse formats, such as a
primer on disaster preparedness for paper-based materials.

Library Support Staff, available at http://www.librarysupportstaff.com.
(accessed 11 May 2008). Extensive, excellent information on both specific and related disaster recovery and emergency management, including policies, procedures, vendors, products, and links (coffee in
libraries, stack management, preservation, repair of objects—film and
video as examples, cleaning and housekeeping recipes, tips and resources for media, hardware, paint, residues for glues, gum and saps,
acid rain, pestilence and droppings, smoke and soot, ink and markers,
cosmetics, rubber/scuff marks, blood oils, tars, and stains from molds
and mildews), housekeeping guidelines, and cleaning information for
food and drink as well as extensive lists of supplies and suppliers.

LOCKSS. Stanford University, Stanford, CA, available at http://www
.lockss.org/lockss/Home (accessed 18 June 2008). Don't miss, unique
(Lots of Copies Keep Stuff Safe) web environment with tools for pre-
serving web content and digital material infrastructure in open source
software for any users.

National Archives and Records Administration, available at http://www
.nara.gov/arch/ (accessed 15 March 2008). Extensive resource offering
content on preservation, management, and training with *A Primer on
Disaster Preparedness, Management and Response: Paper Based Materials*, found at http://www.archives.gov/preservation/emergency-prep/
disaster-prep-primer.pdf.

National Association of School Psychologists (NASP), available at http://
www.nasponline.org/ (accessed 15 March 2008). Don't miss excellent
online resources to help those working with children and youth to
"avoid, prepare for, and cope with crises, tragedies, and disasters of all
kinds."

National Fire Protection Agency, available at http://www.nfpa.org/ (accessed 16 June 2008). Excellent content on the protection of library, museum, historic structure, and archive facilities and collections with a focus on prevention as well as recovery and standards for equipment, roles, and responsibilities of staff with self-inspection checklists and training materials and fact sheets.

National Oceanic and Atmospheric Administration. United States Department of Commerce, available at http://www.noaa.gov/ (accessed 8 May 2008). Content on weather disasters from all weather extremes, safety rules and regulations, conditions caused by extreme weather, including related programs such as "StormReady Program," the *National Weather Service, Natural Hazards Data*, available at http://www.ngdc.noaa.gov/seg/hazard/hazards.shtml and Weather.com, which provides local and regional weather information in a customizable portal and links to the *Family Disaster Supplies Kit.*

The National Organization on Disability. The National Organization on Disability, available at http://www.nod.org/ (accessed 25 June 2008). Extensive content on emergency preparedness and special needs and recommendations for special populations under either "disaster" or "emergency" (although more tangential content is linked under emergency).

National Response Team (NRT). National Response Team (NRT), available at http://www.nrt.org/ (accessed 23 June 2008). Not as likely to be used by libraries but extensive links to hazardous materials with full-text access to fifty-plus fact sheets and planning guides and one hundred-plus links to emergency management and disaster recovery content.

Natural Hazards Center. University of Colorado at Boulder, available at http://www.colorado.edu/hazards/ (accessed 18 June 2008). Don't miss content with full-text articles from diverse sources and access to the free online "HazLit Database," with 22,000-plus items.

North Carolina's Critical Incident Response Kit Project. Center for the Prevention of School Violence, available at http://www.ncdjjdp.org/cpsv/cirk.html (accessed 23 June 2008). Unique content on school violence, including prevention and recovery as well as training for the development of positive attitudes, behaviors, and conditions.

Northern States Conservation Center, available at http://www.collec tioncare.org/cci/cci.html (accessed 8 May 2008). Constantly cited online resource for all types of employees in all types of libraries and related environments with extensive content on preservation principles, designing operating budgets, training staff, equipment, consultants, and storage materials and recommended storage with don't-miss preservation leaflets.

Occupational Safety & Health Administration. U.S. Department of Labor, available at http://www.osha.gov/ (accessed 20 June 2008). Good general data on materials' safety and workplace violence awareness and prevention with great links to http://www.osha-slc.gov/SLTC/ workplaceviolence/, and recommended related communications (www .osha.gov/SLTC/hazardcommunications), valuable newsletters, *OSHA's Job Safety & Health Quarterly*, and fact sheets.

Project School Emergency Response to Violence (SERV). U.S. Department of Education, available at http://www.ed.gov/programs/dvppserv/ index.html (accessed 23 June 2008). Resources designed to assist in services to school districts where learning is disrupted due to school violence and/or crises.

Publications. Conservation Center of Artistic and Historic Artifacts (CCAHA), available at http://ccaha.org/index.php/publications (accessed 23 June 2008). Unusual, excellent content on treatment and training for works of art and artifacts on paper (drawings, prints, maps, posters, historic wallpaper, photographs, rare books, scrapbooks, manuscripts, parchment, and papyrus) with links to consultation services and training through workshops and programs with specific reference to emergency issues.

Ready.gov. Ready.gov. U.S. Dept. of Human Resources, available at http://www.ready.gov/ (accessed 25 June 2008). "Google-like" web search engine for the federal (and related) government content for families and businesses including templates, best practices, recommended emergency kits, and recommendations for communication plans.

SAFE. The School Actions for Emergencies Center. International Society for Technology in Education, available at http://www.eschoolnews.com/ safe-center/about-safe/ (accessed 12 May 2008). K–12 recommendations for campus safety for boards, administrators, faculty, and parents.

Safety and Security Committee. University of Maryland, available at
http://www.lib.umd.edu/PUB/Safety/ (accessed 20 June 2008). Unusual business/institutional approach to address these critical issues,
including a mission and vision statement, roles and responsibilities for
safety and security of library staff, customers, materials, facilities,
equipment, and furnishings; philosophy, policy, or procedure as
needed; training manuals; and coordination and communication
through campus entities.

SafeUSA.org, available at http://safeusa.org/winter.htm (accessed 1 April
2008). Basic information for individuals, families, and businesses on
how to be safe and stay safe during power outages, water shortages,
mass fatalities, civil disturbances, transportation accidents, and building or equipment collapse.

SEFLIN: Southeast Florida Library Information Network, available at
http://www.seflin.org/index.cfm?fuseaction = pages. Disaster available
at http://www.seflin.org (accessed 3 May 2008). Disaster planning,
safety, and recovery resources, including links to best practice and
sample manuals, response plans, policies (for example, lockdown), procedures (for example, hurricanes), and continuity plans.

SOLINET: Southeastern Library Network, available at http://www.solinet
.net/Preservation/Resources%20and%20Publications/
Disaster%20Prevent ion%20Checklist.aspx (accessed 23 June 2008).
Checklists, disaster planning, and prevention content with links to area
resources for bibliographic network members and others.

Threatplan.org. U.S. Department of Justice's Bureau of Alcohol, To-
bacco, Firearms and Explosives (ATF) and the U.S. Department of
Education's Office of Safe and Drug Free Schools, available at
http://www.threatplan.org/ (accessed 23 June 2008). Free, interactive
planning tool for schools training curriculum and recommended resources focused on violence and terrorism.

Time Line Series. Claire Rubin & Associates, Disaster Research and Consulting, 2008, available at http://www.disaster-timeline.com/ (accessed
17 February 2008). Extraordinary don't-miss time lines (free online)
for disasters, terrorism, and homeland security issues.

U.S. Center for Disease Control and Prevention (CDC). U.S. Center for
Disease Control and Prevention (CDC), available at http://www

.cdc.gov/ (accessed 23 June 2008). Health standards, statistics, disease prevention fact sheets, brochures, software, and other publications downloadable for topics on anthrax, botulism, plagues, and smallpox along with an often-cited pandemic flu *Workplace Planning* guide and a unique document from a related organization (National Institute for Occupational Safety and Health (NIOSH) available at http://www.cdc.gov/niosh/. *A Tool Kit to Prevent Senior Falls* for all types and sizes of libraries for legal and liability as well as care and recovery issues.

Web Junction, available at http://www.WebJunction.org (accessed 1 February 2008). Over eighty resources to be used for training, including PPT presentations from conferences.

Yucht, Alice. AliceYucht: Crises Planning Resources. PBWiki. 2008, available at http://aliceyucht.pbwiki.com/CrisisPlanningResources. (accessed 11 May 2008). A don't-miss, wonderful wiki with expanded opportunities for updating (probably the first of many formats on this topic), offering solid content for managers, families, and employees with great, classic links and excellent training curriculum and resource lists.

WHAT'S NOT HERE?

As indicated in the introductory information, hundreds of books and articles and—now thousands—of web resources exist for most disaster and emergency planning and recovery situations. There are a few areas, however, where content is primarily classic in nature and although some of this content can be found in other articles, monographs, and websites, additional and updated content should be created.

Other specific areas excluded primarily included research studies, statistics, vendor lists, .com/consulting environments (unless significant) free and unique online content, thousands of links to institutional plans (unless unique), and policy web environments that included many blogs.

Appendix B

FORM EXAMPLE: MANAGEMENT ISSUES AUDIT

Management Issues Audit

Document Date: _____

Review Date/Revised: _____

Process Owner: _____

Management Issues Audit		
General Management Issues/PROCESS OWNER	*Done/ Will Be Done*	*In Progress*
Is the institution responsible for creating emergency documents? (see Emergency Plan/Disaster Recovery Plan)/LIBRARY DIRECTOR Comments: *Required at institution level with annual review*	*Yes*	*Complete*
Is the Emergency Plan/Disaster Recovery Plan created?/DISASTER TEAM/W/DIRECTOR Comments: *Created in word; need Web document designed*	*Fall '08*	*First draft submitted to system director on 5/2008*
Disseminated?/COMMUNICATIONS DIRECTOR	*Fall '08*	
Kept-up-to-date?/DISASTER TEAM	*March/each year*	*ongoing*
In multiple formats?/DISASTER TEAM	*Print, Web, burned to DVD*	*January '09*
In appropriate languages?/DISASTER TEAM	*English, Spanish*	*January '09*

Appropriate to all constituents including those with special needs? Comments:		
Is the management chain of command accurate and current? Comments:		
Are institutional support mechanisms referenced in Disaster Plans in place and up to date? Comments:		
Insurance?		
Risk management inventories?		
Assess management inventories?		
Evacuation plans?		
Floor plans?		
Are emergency responsibilities and expectations in job descriptions and performance plans laid out? Comments:		
Are budget categories identified for disaster and emergency needs? Comments:		

Are disaster/emergency assessment/evaluation mechanisms in place in the organization? Comments:		
Are training issues articulated and training plans in place? Comments:		
Is the organization environment documented "pre" event/activity? Comments:		
Communication Issues	Done	In-Progress
Is there a communication plan or decision tree for employee communication (contacting each other or their supervisors)? Comments:		
Do employees know how to contact peers and other appropriate individuals in the umbrella institution? Comments:		
Are multiple forms of 24/7 communication contacts available? Comments:		
Has signage been identified, created, and stored for before, during, and after disaster/emergency events/ activities? Comments:		

Does the communication plan include content and training for special needs/special populations? Disabilities		
Non-English speakers		
Do facilities have communication systems such as alarms? Blinking lights? Message boards? Comments:		

FORM EXAMPLE: SPECIAL NEEDS/SPECIAL POPULATIONS AUDIT

Special Needs/Special Populations Audit

Document Date: _____

Review Date/Revised: _____

Process Owner: _____

All content must be gathered in accordance with HIPAA guidelines.

Special Needs/Special Populations Audit		
Issue/PROCESS OWNER	Done/Date	Comments
Have employees with physical or mental limitations self-identified an inability to evacuate the building?/DIRECTOR/ HUMAN RESOURCES		
Have employees with accommodations self-identified disabilities that would necessitate unique assistance during an evacuation?/ HUMAN RESOURCES		

Have employees and employee backups been identified to assist in special needs/ special populations emergency situations?/ HUMAN RESOURCES		
Do training plans include special needs and special populations training?/ DIRECTOR, TRAINING, DISASTER RECOVERY TEAM		
Does training curriculum include special needs and special populations training?/ TRAINING, DISASTER RECOVERY TEAM		
Have self-identified employees with special needs been paired with identified evacuation employees?/HUMAN RESOURCES, TRAINING, DISASTER RECOVERY TEAM		
Do evacuation plans include special needs/ special population equipment? (wheelchairs and other mobility devices?)/HUMAN RESOURCES, BUDGET OFFICERS		
Is there an inventory of special needs, such as language issues? DISASTER RECOVERY TEAM/HUMAN RESOURCES		

FORM EXAMPLE: WHO TO CALL/INFORM

Who to Call/Inform
Contact List/Phone Tree—Natural Disasters

Document Date: _____

Review Date/Revised: _____

Process Owner: _____

Who to Call/Inform					
Location	Name/Title	Primary Contact	Secondary Contact	When to Contact	Comments
Central	Manager, Central Facilities Ray Parker	Work hours cell, text 1-888-453-9878	After hours w/no cell answer 1-446-233-3333	Immediate, first person for natural disasters	Copy e-mail when text is sent.
Carter Branch	Head Librarian Jay Foon	Work hours cell, text 1-354-453-0909	After hours w/no cell answer 1-446-233-3333	Immediate, first person for natural disasters	No e-mail available.
West End Branch	Assistant Head Librarian Bet Sund	Work hours cell, text 1-344-456-0998	After hours w/no cell answer 1-446-233-3333	Immediate, first person for natural disasters	Follow up with pager.

FORM EXAMPLE: CONTACT LIST/PHONE TREE—SECURITY

Contact List/Phone Tree—Security

Document Date: _____

Review Date/Revised: _____

Process Owner: _____

Contact List/Phone Tree—Security					
Location	Name/Title	Primary Contact	Secondary Contact	When to Contact	Comments
Central	Manager, Central Facilities Ray Parker	Work hours cell, text 1-888-453-9878	After hours w/no cell answer 1-446-233-3333	City police, then Ray, Ray contacts media	Copy e-mail when text is sent.
Carter Branch	Head Librarian Jay Foon	Work hours cell, text 1-354-453-0909	After hours w/no cell answer 1-446-233-3333	City police, then Jay, Jay calls Ray.	No e-mail available.
West End Branch	Assistant Head Librarian Bet Sund	Work hours cell, text 1-344-456-0998	After hours w/no cell answer 1-446-233-3333	City police, then Bet, Bet calls Ray.	Follow up with pager.

FORM EXAMPLE: EXPERTS

Experts/Consultants/Resource Specialists
Emergency Management/Disaster Recovery

Document Date: _____

Review Date/Revised: _____

Process Owner: _____

Experts					
Event/ Activity	Expert/ Consultant	Area of Expertise	Contact Information	References	Date Contacted
Hurricane	Dr. Carson Culler	Wet audiovisuals	Dr. Carson Culler 1436 Roadway Washington, DC 20036 CC1224@rr.com 1-202-453-9980	Library of Congress, Frank Ever	2/24/08
	Winona Watcher	Wet print materials	Ms. Winona Watcher 23 Aston K. Street Austin, TX 78757 wwatcher@pp.com 1-512-555-7890	Austin Public Library	3/4/06
Fire	Mr. S. Plugg	Smoke removal, fire damage, soot damage	Plugg, Inc. 12245 Nemo Way Oklahoma City, OK 73101 splugg@hotlink.com 1-405 -455-5556	Director, OK City Public Jen Carter	2/23/03
	Winona Watcher	Wet print materials damaged by fire protection	Ms. Winona Watcher 23 Aston K. Street Austin, TX 78757 wwatcher@oo.com 1-512-555-7890	Austin Public Library	3/4/06
Flood	Dr. Carson Culler	See "hurricane"	See "hurricane"	Library of Congress, Frank Ever	2/24/08
	Winona Watcher	See "hurricane"	See "hurricane"	Austin Public Library	3/4/06

FORM EXAMPLE: SIGN-IN SHEETS/KEEPING/TAKING ROLE

Sign-in Sheets/Keeping/Taking Role
Emergency Management/Disaster Recovery

Event, Activity, Date/Day/Time: _____

Tornado warning 5/6/08; 2:00 p.m. _____

Process Owner: _____

Sign-in Sheets/Keeping/Taking Role					
#	Constituent Name/ Info	Location	Primary Contact/ Relationship	Description/Comments/Issues/ Special Needs	Signature/ Initials
1	Ann Even 45 Way End Dallas, TX 214-657-8989 aeven@rr.com	West End Branch	Mother is Betty Even 214-456-8989 beven@rr.com	Mid-30s brunette Requested non-latex gloves	
2	Billy Even	West End Branch	Grandmother is Betty Even 214-456-8989 beven@rr.com	Six years old Mother requested non-latex gloves	
3					
4					
5					
6					
7					

Review Date/Revised: _____

FORM EXAMPLE: IF/THEN FORMS

If /Then Forms
Emergency Management/Disaster Recovery

Document Date: _____

Review Date/Revised: _____

Process Owner: _____

If/Then Forms			
Event Activity	*Issue*	*If*	*Then*
Tornado Warning	Facility is compromised, such as windows broken, trees down.	*Building is damaged*	*Call facility manager; manager works with media; manager calls police/rescue; manager calls city facilities; asst. manager alerts employees; asst. manager documents scene*
Flood	Water is inside building	*Floor, carpet, furniture, and materials/books are at risk/wet*	*Call facility manager; manager works with media; manager consults vendor list; manager calls city facilities; asst. manager alerts employees; asst. manager documents scene*
Injury Accident	Constituent is injured	*Injury occurs within the building due to emergency/disaster*	*Constituent contact numbers; with permission EMS, facility manager, risk manager; complete accident report forms; complete insurance forms*
Injury Accident	Constituent is injured	*Injury occurs within the building due to constituent accident*	*Constituent contact numbers, with permission EMS, facility manager, risk manager; contact constituent insurance company; complete accident report forms; complete insurance forms*

FORM EXAMPLE: VENDORS

Vendors
Emergency Management/Disaster Recovery

Document Date: _____

Review Date/Revised: _____

Process Owner: _____

Vendors		
Event/Activity/Situation	Vendor Information Contact Information	Comments
Fire	Fire Protection, Inc. 56 Arbor Austin, TX 78701 fpinc@rr.com	Smoke, soot removal; transport to cleaning location; follow-up cleaning crew
	Water Recovery and Associates 3 Artisan Salado, TX 78603 1-516-776-9090 wra@cc.com	Water logged materials dried on-site
	Recovery, Inc. 1st Street, D Level Houston, TX 77006 1-713-999-0909 rl@yu.com	Soot, smoke, general cleaning
Bio/Hazardous Materials	M, M Inc. Aisle Road Raleigh Durham, NC 27703 1-435-666-7777 mmi@ut.com	Mold and mildew treatments, off-site, unique chemical formulary, loading and transportation within quote

EMERGENCY AND DISASTER MANAGEMENT SIGNAGE

Although there are many critical aspects for preparing the environment for emergencies and disasters, the library must have appropriate and required signage relating to emergency management and disaster planning situations. Signage, unique to these situations and created by outside experts or umbrella organization entities or by library staff, can be one of the most important aspects to ensure 'success' and/or safety in difficult times.

The best signage discussion includes public communication and instruction on various of "things" including—but not limited to—walls, doors, hardware, ceilings, floors, handouts, postings (online/websites) as well as assessing styles, colors, typefaces, sizes, and timing for identification, production, storage, and distribution.

Style Checklist Questions			
Entire buildings, areas or departments of buildings, and/or specific services and resources often have unique styles. It is not unusual or inappropriate for environments to choose a style for signage for emergency management and/or disaster planning (EM & D) situations that is completely different from other signage used in the facility. In addition, managers often canvass the nearby neighborhood, the larger community, and/or umbrella organization to determine if other styles or a specific style is used for these unique signs. Given that signs are meant to alert, convey, and indicate status, it stands to reason that signs chosen are consistent.			
Questions	*Yes, Ready to Go (If needed) Placement indicated; storage location indicated*	*Yes, but needs updating*	*No, we need this!*
Do surrounding entities have EM & D signage styles? If so, what is the style of the current EM & D signage to be used?			

Is there a signage system that signage/ content must fit in to/coordinate with?			
Does the style communicate the right message and mood for employees and constituents? Patrons? Customers?			
Do target audiences drive signage variances such as lower reading levels, lower literacy levels, non-English speakers?			
Do current or standard sign configurations drive EM & D designs or choices? (Ex. If community EM & D colors are black and red, but standard library signage is red, how might the library choose complimentary colors that still convey urgency and recommended behaviors?			
Color Checklist Questions			
While colors are important, they also set a tone and a mood as well as consciously and unconsciously direct behaviors.			
Are there colors or color combinations that signal EM & D in the community?			
Are there colors or color combinations that signal EM & D in the neighborhood?			
Are there colors or color combinations that signal EM & D in the umbrella institution?			
Are colors used to define spaces in the library? Are these same colors needed to define spaces in the library in relationship to EM & D (ex. is there a designated shelter area)? Is there a location outside the library—designated by color—where people gather in fire drills and/or bomb scares when evacuated?			
Are color-blind issues for employees? Patrons? Customers? Taken into account when EM &D sign colors are chosen?			

Lighting Checklist Questions

Given EM & D issues with electricity and power (often the "first to go" in EM &D situations), lighting should not be incorporated into the EM & D process unless operated with battery or other alternate energy sources.

Are there alternate energy resources and processes for EM & D elements identified by signage?			
Are there alternate energy resources and processes for EM & D elements identified by instructions? Are these instructions and a timetable for keeping these up-to-date maintained by employees? Management?			
Are library or community safe areas considered in lighting?			
Are safety issues such as steps/stairs needing EM & D lighting?			

Timeliness Checklist Questions

One of the most critical aspects of EM & D is the design and upkeep of signs to identify, direct, alert, and instruct employees, patrons, and others as to what is happening and what to do.

Does sign creation, distribution, and maintenance have appropriate timelines?			
Are signs designed, printed, appropriately labeled, and stored/filed prior to EM & D events (given lack of power and energy losses)?			
Are stored/filed signs on a maintenance list kept up to date?			

Instructions Checklist Questions

Instructions in an increasingly technology-driven service environment are critical to organized, consistent communication delivered to direct behavior critical to success in EM & D general and specific situations. They identify "what has changed" in an environment. Although many can't be specifically or completely designed until the nature of the EM & D situation has been ascertained, instructions, once thought of as "we used to do it this way, but in this EM & D time, please do it THIS way . . ." can be designed as templates or "Swiss cheese" instructions with all but the most important points filled in.

Has the environment been assessed to determine what needs instructions?			

Do instructions attract and then direct the attention needed?			
Do instructions model the appropriate style, etc. of EM & D signage?			
Do instructions both inform as well as direct behavior?			
Special Issues Checklist Questions			
There are always unique aspects to EM & D issues and signage is no exception.			
Has the library considered nametags and other employee identifiers (orange vests, name bands, hats) needed as specific identifiers as signs?			
Are nametags designed to protect employees and patrons, give titles, indicate EM & D responsibilities and offer information yet protect employee services such as "no last names"?			
Are signs accessible by differently-abled customers? Type-size? Braille?			
Are there standards for making and placing signs?			
Is there a signage process owner?			
Are signs in appropriate languages? Do they offer simple "instructions" with universal pictures?			
Are instructions written at the right age level? Reading and/or grade level? In the right language?			
Did/does the signage RFP for general signs include EM & D signage needs?			
Do all departments that have instructions have instruction design for EM & D built in to their responsibilities?			
Is there a backup sign production, timeline, and maintenance timeline available?			
Is there an EM & D process owner?			

Appendix C

VIRTUAL WORLD EMERGENCY SIMULATIONS

Today's virtual world environments are nothing new in both theory and concept. Although more sophisticated and realistic in design and execution, older virtual or "other world" environments have long been used to provide settings for staging, acting out, and working through many situations, including emergency activities.

"Other world" environments used historically include software situations that allow individuals to plan and build cities, towns, and villages as well as activate situations within those environments in order to determine if better plans, designs, training, organization, and so on could obviate or mitigate emergency situations. In addition to this software approach to design, the intellectual process of identifying the environment, establishing the "players," and providing supplies as well as identifying what is *not* in the environment or what is possible to have in the environment, can be called a scenario or case. This is also in print and still considered a popular approach to emergency management decision-making. This typical approach for providing opportunities for decision-making includes:

- Detailed descriptions of "who" the players are (for example, survivors stranded in the basement of a school including a forty-seven-year-old business person, two teenagers, and a retired military man; and three school teachers stranded on a desert island)

- Lists of elements available in the environment (stranded with the survivors is a case of bottled water, twelve packets of beef jerky, a first aid kit, matches, and two flashlights)
- Items not available or missing from the environment (there is no electricity in the building, the plumbing does not appear to be working, and the stairs to the basement door are damaged/ falling down)
- Elements of the situation that are articulated (it appears the earthquake affected a number of buildings nearby, and no rescue crews can be heard to be working yet)

Following the identification of these characteristics of the situation, this process then proposes a series of questions that can be given to an individual to address or to several people who can discuss the variety of ways to address the situation. An individual can then work through the questions, or the group of people can be asked to address the questions. Sample questions for an individual include:

- What should the individuals trapped in the basement do first?
- What are the critical emergency elements of the situation?
- What can be done?
- What can't be done?

The same series of questions can be given to a group of people to address. This activity is designed, with few or no instructions on "how to proceed," to ask the group addressing the situation to decide who they want to "play" or "be" in the activity and then determine answers to the questions. Alternate ways of group problem-solving could include players determined by drawing names or numbers or "roles" from a "hat." When groups answer the questions, the exercise become a multilayered exercise that provides a learning experience that includes:

- How do group members choose characters they will "play" if members are not assigned?
- How is group leadership and management determined for addressing the situation?
- How are group member roles and responsibilities determined?
- What steps should the group leader take first?

Newer virtual world environments (for example, Second Life) provide obvious expanded opportunities and are being used by federal, state, and local emergency management offices and departments. Many other game-playing or gaming environments exist, and these games often simulate role-playing and emergency situations.

ASSESSING READINESS IN VIRTUAL ENVIRONMENTS?

The goal of game or virtual "scoring" is to determine if leaders were chosen in an appropriate manner and if problems were solved or challenges met with the team members playing the roles assigned to them or chosen by them. Additional readiness issues for assessing how the simulation "worked" might include:

- Was there a disaster plan, and if there was a plan, did plan elements assist individuals in making successful decisions?
- Did role players fulfill roles?
- Did role players fulfill responsibilities?
- Were communication plan elements appropriate? Was the media successful?
- Were emergency supplies appropriate?
- Were medical concerns met during the emergency?
- Was training given to groups sufficient?

While some gaming or virtual environments provide opportunities for role players to administer aspects of the game and plot out game changes, other types of software are programmed to move players among disaster elements given choices individuals or groups make. The value of virtual worlds where multiple nongroup members may exist and impact team players includes:

- The challenge presented by the "unknown"
- The opportunity for players to work individually or in teams
- The opportunity (in some environments) for project administrators to change game elements midstream
- The opportunity to produce assessment data systematically and by "outside" parties (such as software-generated data or data that comes from observers or software moderators

Additional virtual emergency environments include virtual state emergency management web environments with 3D simulation and virtual web environments supported by federal entities. Extensive use of simulation also occurs in area-specific emergency management events, such as fire prevention.

One interesting aspect of the virtual emergency management world is the creation of (not simulated or gaming environments) permanent virtual environments. One such environment is typically identified as an emergency operations center, specifically a virtual emergency operations center. These may also be known by their initials EOC and/or VEOC; they may have extensive wireless and satellite networks incorporated into their EOC and may have their own electronic communications list or network. Obviously delivered via the web, these environments are used extensively by the military.